Have A Great Mission!

R. Squires

Life Is
Simple
Hard
But Simple

Life Is
Simple
Hard
But Simple

®

R. TERRY MEISER

Artwork for book cover created by Michael G. Schrack

www.lifeissimplehardbutsimple.com

ISBN - 13: 978-0-9793382-0-5
ISBN - 10: 0-9793382-0-4

First Edition: March 2007
Second Edition: June 2011

Acknowledgements/Dedication

Who shall be included here? My family? Friends? Teachers? Business Associates? Those who assisted me with this book? In any case, the list would be long. My life has been blessed with many people that have assisted me in big and small ways. Sometimes the "small ways" ended up having a major impact. No matter how much thought and effort would be applied, someone would surely be left out much to my regret.

It occurs to me, one unique person would be at the top of nearly every list – my Dad. What a wonderful person he was! He had a rough start in life, but he never left that affect his positive and intense approach to everything he did. Ralph E. Meiser has been gone for over 12 years. The interesting part is he probably has more influence on my life now than when he was alive.

"Dad, this book is dedicated to you."

CONTENTS

INTRODUCTION

Life is Simple?

Life is simple! Are you kidding? Read on. Hard, rock hard, but simple. Don't equate simple with being easy. Well, if you put it that way, maybe, just maybe.

My years have been filled with fascination regarding how hard life can be, all the while convinced that the basic concepts or building blocks [BB's] are fairly easy to comprehend. The work comes in when you try to implement these BB's into your life. For example, Chapter 8, Link 1, "Control What You Think About." Now that makes sense and it's not hard to accept that as a worthy attribute for your life. It is also clear to me that if properly implemented into my life, there would be very little need for the rest of this book. Maybe, and hopefully, it is not that hard for you, but it's a real killer for me.

Pick up any book regarding self-help and the idea of controlling your thoughts will most certainly be mentioned. Most of the BB's presented will likely make sense to you. The biggest difference between the two of us will not be agreeing on the basic BB's, but there will be a lot of variation in where we stand on how they have been implemented into our lives. The intensity level needed for effective implementation will vary greatly. That is how it should be, as we are all unique and all have our very own personal mission to identify and pursue.

My personal belief is that life is not intended to be easy. However, the basics are not that difficult to understand. Everyone can grasp the basics. How hard we are willing to work makes the difference. If you relax and take time to realize and accept that life is intended to be simple – hard, but simple – it is then much easier to appreciate what is going on in your life. You will not find in this book a detailed explanation regarding how you can change any particular area of your life, for example, effective listening, goal-setting, self-esteem, time management, speaking and so forth. The intention is to provide a framework and you can then fill in the voids in your life.

Mountains of very good material exist on most, if not all, of the BB's that will be presented. It is not my goal to "reinvent the wheel" here, but rather to draw your attention to the importance of all the BB's and how they relate. You will not likely find all you need in one book, CD or set of tapes. Many books, CD's and tapes are presented as a cure-all. While they are excellent works, they will only be part of what you need.

What about the Bible? It is the book to end all books, but properly studied it will drive you to all kinds of other places and materials to more fully understand the answers to the three basic questions in life [see Chapter 2], and all that goes along with your development and your personal mission.

There is no need to try to do everything at one time. We are a work in process. You can really get discouraged if you demand too much of yourself in a short period of time. This has been a major stumbling block for me. Having identified something of importance that needs to be accomplished, my response is "why isn't it done?" To gain a better perspective, consider the following story.

A man went to a factory as a visitor. The factory produced very fine pieces of work, one of which was brass doors that went to very stately buildings where the door was the major focal point of the entrance. The visitor followed through the process and when he got down to the end of the line there was a worker who was polishing the doors. He would just work and work on these doors. The visitor walked up to the worker and said "Sir, you are doing a beautiful job here, but how do you know when you're done?" The worker stopped, looked at the visitor and said, "Well, sir, whenever they come and take it away." That is when your mission should be over—when they come and take you away.

Personal Challenges

The only way to feel good about writing this book was to adopt a philosophy of writing it to myself. My implementation comes up way too short in many areas of my life, making it difficult to think about telling someone else how they should live their life. By accepting this approach, it was clear that it fits the overall concept that is presented. It is my hope and prayer that we will both benefit.

Another problem in writing this book was to remain true to the "simple" approach. I had trouble coming up with much to say about several areas of major importance. The short paragraphs seemed to be all that was needed. However, I would persist in trying to add words that only seemed to cloud what was already clearly said. What assured me not to worry about needing to add words was realizing the manner in which the Bible was written. There are many profound statements and ideas in the Bible that take very few words to convey. It seems to me many people have trouble accepting something unless there are paragraphs written to make it appear important. There are very brief comments made, again from the Bible, that open the door for us to gain a lot of understanding. We should take advantage instead of assuming it must not be important because so little was said.

One-to-One

Ask any teacher and they will verify that the larger the class, the more difficult the teaching process becomes, all the while the students are learning less.

My most vivid experience with this was observing my son spending a year attending Valley Forge Military College and then transferring to Penn State University. While both schools excel as learning institutions, it was clear that the very small classes, in some cases single-digit size, at Valley Forge provided an enhanced opportunity for the individual student. Of course, this was at a drastic increase in cost.

In writing this book, my primary goal is to write it to myself. Hopefully, you will get the one-to-one feel as you study what is presented.

Workbook Approach

Keeping with the overall theme, this is not intended to be an "end all" or final version of anything. The format is a workbook style. My personal intention is to use this as a framework which will be built upon and adjusted during the rest of my life. As you work with this framework, feel free to make it your own. You are unique, and therefore this book should be unique to you and your own personal mission in life.

The chapter on Subjects to Study is an area where you will probably benefit by adding and subtracting freely to properly reflect you and your growth in the future. Plan to have pen in hand every time you pick this up and make notes without restraint. It is certainly not my intention to preach a sermon here. This framework and the BB's have worked for me; hopefully, they will serve as a guide for you.

Building Blocks

There are a lot of concepts, ideas and subjects covered throughout this book. For lack of a better term, let's just call them building blocks [BB's]. Every one of these BB's should stand alone. None of the BB's should conflict with any of the others. Properly described, understood and implemented, they should enhance each other. There will be a synergistic effect multiplied many times over as you improve each BB. With this in mind, the book can be read forward, backward or inside-out.

You vs. "Things"

While there is nothing inherently wrong by getting "things," that subject is not what we are going to consider. Things may well be important, but only as one aspect of your life. What we become is far more important and will be the overall emphasis of this discussion.

My Objective

My objective with this book is not to convince you to think like me, but rather to convince you to challenge the way you think. Let's get started.

Part I

What Is This All About?

CHAPTER 1

My Guidance System

Everyone has a philosophy that governs their life whether they are aware of it or not. This chapter is not intended to cover my entire philosophy, but the seven areas discussed have and will continue to have a profound impact on how my life unfolds. They represent a basic framework of guidance that has meaningful impact on the message contained in this book. You may or may not agree with my approach and conclusions in these areas. However, understanding where I'm coming from may better enable you to benefit from the information presented in this book.

Religious Beliefs

On the subject of religion, you can put me down as being pleased, proud and humble to be a Christian. Yes, a non-Church going Christian. The subject of not going to Church will have to be addressed in another book. Is it my position that you will go to Hell if you are not a Christian? No, absolutely not! Does your going to Church offend me as a waste of time? No, absolutely not!

Religion is a sensitive and explosive subject. It took a lot of time and energy for me to get comfortable with my beliefs on this important aspect of life. One of the most difficult areas for me involved accepting that your "being on a different page" is not only okay, but it is exactly where you should be.

It is not my intent to offend you on this issue, but you should be aware of my position, on perhaps the most important area of anyone's life.

Change

We all fight change and you have to wonder at times if it's really necessary. It's very difficult to think about life without realizing the process of life is all about change. From the moment we were born, we were changing. The process of change continues, for good or bad, until we die. To the best of my knowledge, there is no aspect of life where this is not true.

The process of change includes physical, emotional, social, financial, educational, spiritual and every other aspect of life. Your priorities – mine are faith, family, friends, fitness and financial – should not change; however, they will certainly be challenged and affected, as change assaults the many areas of your life. What should concern you is feeling no need to change and/or believing that you are not changing. Saying no to change or the desire to change is basically saying "I'm perfect." Don't allow yourself to get caught up in that deadly trap.

So how should we approach change? It happens everyday-- something comes along and smacks you right in the face and says "you need to change." Our first and natural reaction is to reject whatever it is that confronts us. We lead with our emotions, and they can be powerful. Don't be put off by this reaction on your part, because we are built that way. We have a right to our emotions, don't we? Yes, of course. However, we also have a responsibility to challenge our emotions. This is where the rub comes into play. We feel "we are right" and now our feelings have been challenged and maybe even insulted. The challenge doesn't make you, it reveals you at that moment in your life, and it may be revealing that you need to change.

What should we do? First, accept your feelings but don't be overwhelmed. Second, consider the challenge at hand and look at it carefully to see if, in fact, you might need to adjust your thinking or beliefs. This requires good self-esteem on your part and a keen desire to improve yourself. Third, taking an honest look at the facts and options will confirm either (1) there is no need to adjust or change; or (2) there is indeed a need to learn and grow by changing in this area of your life. Fourth, making the change may feel awkward and scary at first. However, the good news is that in a short while, your feelings will adjust and in the future, the old way of feeling will be what is uncomfortable. When challenged to go back to the old way, you can feel confident in saying to yourself, "I've been there before, and have now found a better way to deal with this part of my life." After you use this approach for a period of time and benefit from the process and results, you will not be uncomfortable when challenged in the future. The process outlined is simple, but it can be very hard to accept until you see how beneficial it can be in helping you accept and implement change when change comes along. If you accept that change is always going to be part of your life and adopt a positive approach to dealing with change, you can go forward, looking forward to the process and benefits of change.

Learn from the past . . .

Live in the present . . .

Prepare for the future . .

It's all about change.

<u>Research</u>

In researching anything in the Bible, my approach has been to use clear statements and ideas to understand unclear statements and ideas. Using this approach also works well for me regarding life in general. Life and the Bible unfold and become much more understandable for me using this strategy.

Observing people trying to explain away clear statements with unclear information has plagued me since my earliest days. It always seemed, and still does, that people were trying to reinforce their established beliefs and positions, rather than trying to learn, grow and unlock secrets that would better help them answer the three basic questions of life. It's like trying to put a puzzle together by forcing the pieces to fit. Not forcing issues really takes the stress out of life. It may not make you very popular with other people or organizations; however, that should not be your personal mission. My approach is to work through whatever comes up and try to stay well-directed, balanced and focused.

The "Yeah Yeah" Factor

We are all guilty of "yeah yeah, I've heard it all before" or "yeah yeah, I know how to do that," "yeah yeah" this and "yeah yeah" that. It is easy for me to get annoyed with others when trying to help them by presenting an idea, and their response is "yeah yeah." What they really want is to get the floor and tell you more than they know.

A recent experience with a gentleman I met seems to sum it up for me. It was disastrous to ask him a question or make a statement because he would spend the next 15 or 20 minutes, or as much time as I would give him, telling me more than he knew. It was just "yeah yeah" and he would go from there. Falling into this trap is far too easy and should be guarded carefully.

As you go through the chapters in this book and the various BB's, they are put together a little differently. Perhaps it is best to just say you may have heard it all before, but the point is you need to focus and realize how important these simple ideas really are in determining your future development. It will not be easy but it will be well worth any amount of effort. Some areas are obviously easier for some people, and vice versa. Make every effort not to fall into the "yeah yeah" trap and find yourself not benefiting from good ideas here or anywhere else in your life.

Hustle

Many years ago, my possessions included a button routinely worn on my cap that simply read "HUSTLE!" Several years after acquiring this button, my family was on a vacation at the shore. There was a shop on the boardwalk where you could make your own buttons, so I made a number of them and took them back home. They were just handwritten on different colors of paper. Now having these "hustle" buttons, something needed to be done with them. What developed was a "hustle" button program for my employees. It worked out very well, and we continued it as long as the business was in operation.

The program worked like this:
1. Every week at our Thursday staff meeting, each of the managers could nominate employees for a "hustle" button.
2. The group, usually just three of us, would consider the names and decide who, if anyone, would be awarded a button. There was no set number to be handed out.
3. The recipients would be told by their manager to "see the boss." The first few times several of the employees balked at having to see the boss. Very quickly it caught on, and they were happy to get the reward and spend a few minutes one-on-one with the boss.
4. The important point here is the only competition was with themselves, not with each other. The employee could qualify to be considered by not missing any time or having any safety violations that week.

5. What we were looking for was some extra hustle on the part of that employee. Did they spot a problem, solve a problem or go out of their way somehow that was over and above what they were expected to do? Many buttons were awarded to employees that were there week after week doing a consistently good job.

6. After wearing the button for a week (and many did not want to wear them), they would give it back and get a small cash reward which I just paid out of my pocket.

The benefits of this program were absolutely outstanding. Everyone knew that they were being watched for something they did right, and that made all the difference in the world. The positive effect on the employees, managers and the business was hard to believe. The program was a huge success because it was simple, easy to understand, consistent and focused only on what the employees did right. Each person was competing with themselves, not with anyone else, and they were very well aware that was the case.

- Everyone knows there are others who are better than they are in many ways.
- Everyone needs to know and believe that doing better is possible, recognized and rewarded.
- Everyone can do better.
- Everyone appreciates recognition.
- Everyone gets enough negative feedback elsewhere.
- <u>Everyone can hustle</u>!

The intent here is to get you to compete or "hustle," not with others but with yourself. You will need to generate your own rewards, but when you get it rolling, it can become very addictive.

<u>The Until Theory</u>

The "Until Theory" is simply this – you just say, well, I'm going to work with this, I'm going to focus on this, its going to be part of me <u>until</u> I'm successful. This idea resulted from attending a seminar where a gentleman by the name of Les Brown talked about playing a game with his son. I do not recall what the game was, but it doesn't matter. Les wanted to go to bed and his son said "No, Dad, it's not over <u>until</u> I win." He made quite a big thing about it and did it very effectively. Yogi Berra might put it a different way – "it's not over until it's over."

Life is not necessarily a matter of winning, but there is an element of winning involved. When you compete in a sporting event, in order for you to win, someone else has to lose. For someone else to win, you have to lose. Life doesn't need to be that way. <u>We can all win</u>!

Proofs

When considering any subject important enough to be included in your life, it is necessary to have anchors. The anchors confirm and validate your position. For me to be completely comfortable, two anchors need to be in place — (1) the attribute is generally appreciated and expected in other people; and (2) a clear statement exists in the Bible to anchor my position, which I call Biblical Anchors.

Everything included in this book has, from my perspective, the first anchor in place. The Biblical Anchors are listed in Appendix I; however, you will need to look them up for your own edification. You may find it very helpful to read several translations. Being an amateur on the Bible, while being confident they exist, many of these Biblical Anchors are missing. If you know where they are, please fill them in and feel free to forward the information, and I thank you in advance.

My <u>Guidance System</u> is:

Notes/Comments:

CHAPTER 2

The Three Basic Questions of Life

1. *Where did I come from?*
2. *Why am I here?*
3. *Where am I going?*

Years ago, I believed these questions offered no more than interesting comments about the subject of life. When I seriously considered them, they got a real grip on me.

There is really not that much to comment on other than to emphasize these three simple questions are dynamite when it comes to understanding the meaning of your life. There will be plenty for you to consider when you really explore these areas deeply and sincerely. If you ignore a serious response to these three questions, life becomes much tougher and will have less meaning. It is vital for you to answer these questions. Not doing so will leave you spinning in the wind.

We all came from somewhere and we are all going somewhere regardless of what you do about anything, including how you deal with question no. 2 above. While this book deals primarily with question no. 2, a clear understanding of its answer will most likely require a lot of soul-searching concerning questions 1 and 3.

Notes/Comments:

CHAPTER 3

Personal Mission

Begin With the End in Mind

The 99 building blocks in Part 2 lead up to and support your personal mission. Why, then, is the Personal Mission coming first? Steven Covey's book, <u>The Seven Habits of Highly Effective People</u>, says it as well as anything I've ever read or heard – "begin with the end in mind." Remember, you can read this book forward, backward or inside out. Therefore, it may be a very good idea to come back to this chapter when you are finished, as well as from time to time in the future. The basic premise of this book is to determine your very own personal mission and then discuss what it will take on your part to achieve the mission you have set before yourself.

What Is a Personal Mission?

It is not a goal. While it could easily be considered a long-term goal, there are definite differences between the two. A goal should be established with a deadline. Unless you know the date of your departure from this earth, your personal mission does not have or need a deadline.

Goals can be independent of each other; however, they should all support your single personal mission. A goal should be out-of-reach but not out-of-sight. A properly stated personal mission would be simple and easy to understand, but most likely it will be elusive and very hard to ever feel you are actually closing in on its conclusion. Goals should be flexible; they can be adjusted and in some cases dropped all together. If your personal mission is properly thought out and stated, you should not have to constantly adjust and question its existence in your life.

The essence of a good personal mission:

- It should be clear, concise, brief, direct, simple and personal. Evaluate every word—-words are powerful.
- It should not conflict with other areas of your life. Rather, it should work hand-in-hand and be supported by everything else in your life, starting with the 99 building blocks in Part 2.

- If it appears as a problem to be resolved, trust me, it's the wrong one.
- It should feel very comfortable (right for you) and not be driving you to find the conclusion. Rather, it should <u>draw</u> you each and every day of your life to become the person you need to be to adequately fulfill your personal mission.
- It should describe who you are and what you are about.
- Remember—life is simple; hard, but simple. It stands to reason that your personal mission should be simple but not easy.
- Be careful not to include the need to change other people to feel you are succeeding. You will have a big enough job making the necessary changes in your own life.

The bottom line is this — your personal mission should describe the number one reason you are alive. In other words, it should answer life's number two question—why am I here? Science has adequately demonstrated that no two of us are alike. While it makes sense to me that we are all here for the same basic reason, we are unique in another way – we each have a different personal mission.

<u>Why Is a Personal Mission Important</u>?

If you are going to be motivated, you need something to be motivated about. Successful people and people in the process of succeeding need to have a burning desire. It is often easy to sell ourselves short and settle for something just okay.

The book by Jim Collins, <u>From Good to Great</u>, is full of good illustrations of people who did not settle for good; unfortunately, many do. The statement "good is the enemy of great" is perhaps the point Collins made that sticks with me best. Properly directed, balanced and focused, we can achieve extraordinary things with our lives. Mark Twain hit the nail on the head when he said "Inherently, each one of us has the substance within to achieve whatever our goals and dreams define. What is missing from each of us is the training, education, knowledge and insight to utilize what we already have."

The major benefit in going through the process of establishing a personal mission is all the things you will learn along the way. After completing my accounting degree at Penn State, I found myself working as a staff accountant for a large accounting firm in Buffalo,

NY. Not being very experienced, especially in the tax area, staff accountants would often go to the Tax Department to get answers. The Tax Manager's response was "well, there's the library. Look it up." Believing we were on the same team, that would always frustrate me. Why should my time be wasted when he already knew the answer? After a while, his real intentions became apparent. He was actually doing me a favor. By doing the research myself, many other related and sometimes unrelated items would be picked up in the process. Each time, instead of discovering the answer to one question, other information would be garnered. At that time, the process was not very appealing, but his approach was certainly correct.

To live life fully, you need an overwhelming mission to draw out the best you have to offer.

How do you go about Creating a Personal Mission?

Are you to create or find your personal mission? Excellent question. And it's up for debate just like "which came first, the chicken or the egg?" Does it really matter? Not to me. If it matters to you, then work on the answer, but don't get so carried away that you lose sight of the more important issue concerning what is your personal mission. There is no need to reinvent the wheel as far as the process is concerned. Tons of material exist to aid and guide you. The important point is don't confuse the process with the outcome you are after, which is the creation of something new and unique—your personal mission.

You need to look deep, very deep, inside yourself and fully understand where you are at this moment. That is something only you can do. At that point, you can then begin to design the mission and the strategy to pursue and achieve your selected task. Realize this is a wonderful challenge, perhaps even a "riddle" into which you can immerse yourself.

Choosing your personal mission does not need to be stressful. However, it should be done carefully and with deliberation. It is your personal mission, and you should be the one taking the responsibility to make the decisions for its creation. We are all blessed with the power to choose in many areas of our lives. As the ramifications of the choices become greater, it is imperative that we make correct choices. You may not like the choices, but you will always have a choice.

Perhaps the most difficult aspect of developing my own mission was to accept just how simple and straight-forward it really turned out to be. This may sound strange, but I was literally trying to develop my mission for years.

Problem-solving for me has always meant finding a quiet spot, getting out a blank piece of paper, and allowing the ideas to flow. In preparation for these sessions, I would read, listen to tapes, meditate on the subject, and after finding a quiet place and securing paper and pen, I would proceed to create absolutely nothing. As a side venture, usually a very concise thought would cross my mind, which would be immediately dismissed as being entirely too simple. Something as important as my mission would certainly be grand and require a lot of time, energy, and pen and paper to create. Pen and paper always worked for me, but I could never even get started. The only result would be a few words that sounded very canned and unfit for the subject at hand, but nothing of substance. After working for extended periods of time trying to come up with something, the paper was still blank. Reading others' missions did not work. Reading company mission statements was even less beneficial. Entire sets of tapes on the subject concerning how to prepare a mission were consumed. Nothing worked.

It reminded me of an event that happened while taking the CPA exam back in May of 1968. There was only one place in the entire exam where we had a choice of questions to answer. Knowing almost nothing, or very little, about the one question, the other appeared possible. After struggling with the problem for what seemed like an hour, nothing was accomplished. My mind just shut down on that subject. Very reluctantly, I switched over to the other problem. The results of that problem are forever hidden. I am grateful it does not matter, having passed the exam and being able to forget the "freeze-up."

At some point, I started paying attention to the thought that would cross my mind. It did not take very long until I began to realize that this was it. This was my mission. The more I meditated on this idea, the more it made sense and fit me perfectly. The title of this book had been in my mind for years. Now I realize that even when considering the documentation and verbalization of my mission, the keystone of my life, it, too, was so simple--hard, but simple, that I had dismissed it for years. Every day since the acceptance of this mission statement I have considered it and looked toward its implementation. Something is drawing, not pushing, me.

Was all my effort a waste of time? No. The side benefits were worth all the time and money expended. My point is this – you can make a lot of progress by just paying attention and DON'T MISS THE OBVIOUS.

Keys to Implementing Your Personal Mission

The key to a successful personal mission is in the implementation. You start with the knowledge and understanding of what it will be and why, but the real benefit comes in seeing the mission <u>becoming</u> a success. Consider these points:

- Here's the first step – start right where you are. "Go as far as the eye can see. When you get there, you will see even further." Napoleon Hill. It is like driving a car at night.
- Make it part of you.
- Consider adopting a definition of success discussed in Chapter 12, which is—the progressive realization of a worthy ideal. In this case, your personal mission.
- You need to believe and accept your personal mission will count in the greater scheme of things. Maybe not in your lifetime, but in the end it will count. You will have made a difference.
- Consider this a lifelong process. It will alleviate the day-to-day pressure and allow you to focus on one day at a time. You have the rest of your life, and nobody has more time than that.
- Enjoy the process—the journey. It is hard to appreciate the destination if you did not enjoy the journey.
- Continue to read, pray, meditate, listen and interact with others, always searching for ways to improve the implementation process.
- Learn to use small amounts of time. See Link 13.
- Keep an open mind. You can only make progress if you are willing to challenge, not necessarily change, what already

exists in your life.

- When you see something that is not working and serving you well anymore – change. Take the new understanding and run with the knowledge that you have found a better way.
- Your success depends on many things, but mostly on **YOU**.
- Believe that you will not regret giving this your very best effort.
- Accept that you must become a different person to accomplish your personal mission. That is what Part 2 is all about.

Can You Change Your Personal Mission?

Of course you can change your personal mission if you feel that is necessary. Properly set, chances are you will never feel the need to make any changes. Please note there will undoubtedly be many things to change in your life. Most likely, if you feel your personal mission needs change, careful analysis will reveal one or more of the building blocks need to be adjusted, not your personal mission. In any case, remember it is your mission and it does not belong to anyone else. It is entirely possible you will not get it set clearly the first time. Do not saddle yourself with something that does not fit. If necessary, adjust or completely change your personal mission.

Should You Share Your Personal Mission With Others?

A means of gaining commitment on your part would be to share your personal mission with other people. However, it will be easier to change or adjust if you have not shared it with others. Your mission is YOURS. It is not mine, and it does not belong to someone else. It is not right or wrong. Being solely yours, you are solely responsible for the pursuit and accomplishment of this unique task. You do not have to share your mission with anyone else if you choose not to. Neither do you have to report to anyone on your progress. It may be very beneficial to share your mission, or aspects of it, with others, but think carefully before you have a wholesale discussion with a lot of people. Others may very well not share your interests or have any real concern for you. They most certainly will not be able to appreciate your enthusiasm and commitment to something they did not help create.

My experience has been that it works best to share only with someone you really trust, who is in a position to help you, and has a reason to do so. Your personal mission is intended to be personal. Perhaps you should not share it at all.

My <u>Personal Mission</u> is:

Notes/Comments:

Part II

Building Blocks [BB's]

CHAPTER 4

Pillars

1.	Appreciation	13.	Industry
2.	Character	14.	Joy
3.	Compassion	15.	Kindness
4.	Contentment	16.	Love
5.	Discipline	17.	Patience
6.	Faith	18.	Peace
7.	Faithfulness	19.	Proactiveness
8.	Forgiveness	20.	Resolution
9.	Frugality	21.	Responsibility
10.	Generosity	22.	Service
11.	Honesty	23.	Silence
12.	Humility	24.	Tolerance

25. Wisdom

Do these pillars describe you? What do they say about you? They are not something you just think about and consider. They are part of your life. Actually, they are part of your very being. They are not something you agree with; they are what you do and become. Everything about you rests on these pillars. Therefore, they must be rock solid. It is important to understand these subjects well--how they are simple and how they are complex. How they can stand alone and how they work together and reinforce each other. Strive for balance and good integration with all the other BB's. The major difference between Subjects to Study [STS] and Pillars involves adding and subtracting from the list. You can add or subtract freely from the STS without affecting who you are. While I would recommend adding to the list of Pillars if you want, please think carefully before you reduce the number on the list presented. This stuff is forever.

PILLAR 1 - APPRECIATION

- Everyone appreciates appreciation.
- Webster's definition – "to grasp the nature, worth, quality or significance of."
- We all need each other; therefore, it makes sense we should appreciate others AND let them know we do.
- Don't discount a small gift of "thank you" or a smile as a means to show appreciation.
- Practice showing appreciation every day.
- Be sure you graciously accept appreciation that is offered to you.
-
-
-
-
-
-
-
-

1. On a scale of 1-10, how do you rate yourself on this issue?
2. Why is this important in your life?
3. If you were to improve in this area, how would it affect your life?
4. Who can help you? Perhaps as a role model?
5. What is the first step you will take?
6. When will you begin?
7. Where [on a scale of 1-10] do you want to be a year from now?

PILLAR 2 - CHARACTER

- To the degree they are part of your life, perhaps the whole list of Pillars could be said to represent your character.
- Like your personality, your character is not easy to change, especially from someone else's point of view. Perception is reality; therefore, it is vital to protect your character like life itself.
- Character and reputation are not the same, although they are close. Character is who you really are, while reputation is what people believe you are.
- Many years ago, my Father told me, "guard your reputation because, good or bad, it goes out in front of you." He was correct.
- A lifetime of work to create a good reputation can be upset with one bad decision.
- Perception is reality, so guard your reputation as you build your character.
-
-
-
-
-

1. On a scale of 1-10, how do you rate yourself on this issue?
2. Why is this important in your life?
3. If you were to improve in this area, how would it affect your life?
4. Who can help you? Perhaps as a role model?
5. What is the first step you will take?
6. When will you begin?
7. Where (on a scale of 1-10) do you want to be a year from now?

PILLAR 3 – COMPASSION

- Webster's definition – "sympathetic consciousness of other's distress together with a desire to alleviate it."
- There are times when people just need someone who cares, knowing there is nothing that can be done to alleviate the situation.
- In every situation, you can be compassionate and you can pray with or for the person that needs your help. Effective listening skills are golden in difficult times.
- Lack of compassion casts a light on how others perceive you in a way that turns people off.
- Sincere compassion is a good way to shed barriers between yourself and others.
- People don't care how much you know until they know how much you care.
-
-
-
-
-
-

1. On a scale of 1-10, how do you rate yourself on this issue?
2. Why is this important in your life?
3. If you were to improve in this area, how would it affect your life?
4. Who can help you? Perhaps as a role model?
5. What is the first step you will take?
6. When will you begin?
7. Where (on a scale of 1-10) do you want to be a year from now?

PILLAR 4 – CONTENTMENT

- We are wired to strive for more; however, don't let striving create strife in your life.
- Learn to be content with what you have while you are pursuing what you want.
- If you are not content now, "more" of anything will not produce lasting contentment.
- Learning to be content with who you are, where you are, and what you have opens the door to happiness and fulfillment in your life.

-
-
-
-
-
-
-
-

1. On a scale of 1-10, how do you rate yourself on this issue?
2. Why is this important in your life?
3. If you were to improve in this area, how would it affect your life?
4. Who can help you? Perhaps as a role model?
5. What is the first step you will take?
6. When will you begin?
7. Where (on a scale of 1-10) do you want to be a year from now?

PILLAR 5 – DISCIPLINE

- Discipline in your thinking, your words and your actions.
- Discipline is one thing; self-discipline is quite another.
- There are many places in our society where we are subject to discipline. The military is a good example.
- The work place requires we act and produce within a framework of discipline.
- If your discipline disappears when the authority and control over you disappears, you do not have much discipline.
- How you respond to life's demands when you are not subject to a framework of outside discipline is what really counts.
- Discipline refined is self-discipline.
- Freedom is what we all want. Accepting the responsibility that comes with freedom requires a lot of self-discipline.
- Self-discipline is a beautiful thing to observe in another person, best of all in yourself.
- Self-discipline will leave your conscious clear at the end of the day.
- Perseverance requires self-discipline and will pay big dividends.
- Self-discipline is worth much more than insight and knowledge. Without self-discipline, you will not persevere long enough to benefit from your good insight and knowledge.
-
-
-

---

1. On a scale of 1-10, how do you rate yourself on this issue?
2. Why is this important in your life?
3. If you were to improve in this area, how would it affect your life?
4. Who can help you? Perhaps as a role model?
5. What is the first step you will take?
6. When will you begin?
7. Where (on a scale of 1-10) do you want to be a year from now?

PILLAR 6 - FAITH

- The subject of faith is a mystical concept to most people. If we substitute or add the idea of belief and/or confidence, suddenly faith becomes more tangible.

- Faith implies belief, confidence and conviction in a situation. You can have *faith* in something, you can *believe* in something, you can have *confidence* in something and you can KNOW it is true. When you consider these points long enough, the lines begin to blur. It may be best not to consider faith as a completely separate issue.

- The separation of faith and belief for most people seems to hinge on being able to prove with facts that something is true. If one is short on facts, they may have faith but not belief. I prefer to look at it a little differently. My faith/belief may not be backed up with facts to prove it to another person, but I am satisfied with the situation. Plus, I am always looking for facts and whatever I can to clarify my faith/belief on a particular subject.

- Fundamental for this to work long-term is a willingness to change what you believe (what you have faith in) when you get new information that clearly points out you need to adjust your position. Having faith does not absolve you from the responsibility to search, consider and adjust when necessary. I have had absolute faith in things I now know were absolutely wrong.

-

1. On a scale of 1-10, how do you rate yourself on this issue?
2. Why is this important in your life?
3. If you were to improve in this area, how would it affect your life?
4. Who can help you? Perhaps as a role model?
5. What is the first step you will take?
6. When will you begin?
7. Where (on a scale of 1-10) do you want to be a year from now?

PILLAR 7 - FAITHFULNESS

- Being unfaithful in any situation will deal a blow that is nearly impossible to recover from. At the least, you will need to work overtime to have any hope of correcting the situation.
- Being faithful to yourself is just as important as being faithful to others.
- You can apply being faithful to all the other Pillars – from being faithful in appreciating what others do for you to being faithful in your pursuit of wisdom.

-
-
-
-
-
-
-
-

1. On a scale of 1-10, how do you rate yourself on this issue?
2. Why is this important in your life?
3. If you were to improve in this area, how would it affect your life?
4. Who can help you? Perhaps as a role model?
5. What is the first step you will take?
6. When will you begin?
7. Where (on a scale of 1-10) do you want to be a year from now?

PILLAR 8 - FORGIVENESS

- We all make mistakes and need to be forgiven.
- Sometimes the hardest person to forgive is yourself.
- For someone to be truly forgiven, they need to ask for forgiveness.
- If you sincerely ask for forgiveness, you will seldom be turned away, and if you are, the responsibility is now on the other person, not you.
- Real healing cannot take place in a relationship until forgiveness is asked for and received.
- How does all this work? I have no clue, but it works!
-
-
-
-
-
-
-
-

1. On a scale of 1-10, how do you rate yourself on this issue?
2. Why is this important in your life?
3. If you were to improve in this area, how would it affect your life?
4. Who can help you? Perhaps as a role model?
5. What is the first step you will take?
6. When will you begin?
7. Where (on a scale of 1-10) do you want to be a year from now?

PILLAR 9 - FRUGALITY

- Webster's definition of frugal is "characterized by or reflecting economy in the expenditure of resources."
- Frugality can be equated to being responsible.
- This has nothing to do with the political version of conservative and liberal.
- Frugality does not refer only to money.
- This does not mean you should be "cheap."
- A fool and his money (resources) are soon parted (but they make a great date)!
- Be especially frugal with the expenditure of your time. This is the one resource you have no hope of ever getting back. Loss of money, health, family, friends, property, etc. may be difficult to replace, but it is possible. NOT so with time.
-
-
-
-
-
-

---

1. On a scale of 1-10, how do you rate yourself on this issue?
2. Why is this important in your life?
3. If you were to improve in this area, how would it affect your life?
4. Who can help you? Perhaps as a role model?
5. What is the first step you will take?
6. When will you begin?
7. Where (on a scale of 1-10) do you want to be a year from now?

PILLAR 10 - GENEROSITY

- Not just with money.
- Being generous with your time is for many people more difficult than being generous in other ways.
- We are all blessed in various ways except with time. We all have the same 24 hours in a day. Therefore, being generous with time is like giving others part of yourself.
- Become known for being a generous person, but not a patsy. Balance is important here like everywhere else.
-
-
-
-
-
-
-
-

1. On a scale of 1-10, how do you rate yourself on this issue?
2. Why is this important in your life?
3. If you were to improve in this area, how would it affect your life?
4. Who can help you? Perhaps as a role model?
5. What is the first step you will take?
6. When will you begin?
7. Where (on a scale of 1-10) do you want to be a year from now?

PILLAR 11 - HONESTY

- Don't kid yourself—we are all guilty of failing in this area on occasion.
- It is easier in the long run to deal with the truth, even if you do not like doing so.
- If you are honest, you do not have to remember what you said.
- You are either an honest person or you are not. That does not necessarily mean you never mess up. But when you do, you own up to it immediately.
- This does not mean you should create problems for others by giving truthful information that will only do harm and serve no positive purpose.
- One of the commandments says we should not bear <u>false witness</u>. Think about this and remember all the other points in the book (Pillars and beyond) as you develop this point and apply it in your life regarding kindness, love, silence...
- First and foremost, be honest with yourself.
-
-
-
-

---

1. On a scale of 1-10, how do you rate yourself on this issue?
2. Why is this important in your life?
3. If you were to improve in this area, how would it affect your life?
4. Who can help you? Perhaps as a role model?
5. What is the first step you will take?
6. When will you begin?
7. Where (on a scale of 1-10) do you want to be a year from now?

PILLAR 12 - HUMILITY

- True humility is a sign of strength not weakness.
- We all need each other and get more than we deserve in life.
- It is okay to be proud, but be humble in the process.
- Strive to understand this pillar deeply.
-
-
-
-
-
-
-
-
-
-

1. On a scale of 1-10, how do you rate yourself on this issue?
2. Why is this important in your life?
3. If you were to improve in this area, how would it affect your life?
4. Who can help you? Perhaps as a role model?
5. What is the first step you will take?
6. When will you begin?
7. Where (on a scale of 1-10) do you want to be a year from now?

PILLAR 13 - INDUSTRY

- Webster on industry says "diligence in an employment or pursuit; a systematic labor especially for the useful purpose with the creation of something of value."
- You can look up "industry" in Webster's dictionary of synonyms. It will be worth your while. A good understanding of the word will put some PUNCH into your work and how you expend your time.
- Many years ago, I picked up a little pamphlet which was about 3½" x 4 ½". On the outside it said, "The secret of how to make money." On the inside, it said "go to work." On the back was a definition of work as follows:

WORK

If you are poor . . . work.
If you are rich . . . continue to work.
If you are burdened with seemingly unfair
    responsibilities . . . work.

If you are happy . . . keep right on working.
Idleness gives wrongful doubts and fears.
If disappointments come . . . work.
If sorrow overwhelms you and loved ones are
    not true . . . work.

When faith falters and reason fails . . . just work.
When dreams are shattered and hope seems dead . . . work.
Work as if your life were in peril.
It really is.

No matter what ails you . . . work.
Work faithfully . . . work with faith.
Work is the greatest remedy available.
Work will cure both mental and physical afflictions.

Thank God every morning when you get up that you have something to do which must be done whether you like it or not.

Being forced to work, and forced to do your best will breed in you temperance, self-control, diligence, strength of will, content, and a hundred other virtues which the idle will never know.

-

-

-

-

-

-

-

-

-

-

-

1. On a scale of 1-10, how do you rate yourself on this issue?
2. Why is this important in your life?
3. If you were to improve in this area, how would it affect your life?
4. Who can help you? Perhaps as a role model?
5. What is the first step you will take?
6. When will you begin?
7. Where (on a scale of 1-10) do you want to be a year from now?

- Life without joy is very difficult.
- Have a passion for whatever you are doing.
- Look for happiness in everything you do and everywhere you go.
- You cannot have a fulfilled life without being happy.
- Would you rather be around someone who is joyful or despondent?
- You can choose to be full of joy, happiness and hope by focusing on what is good in your life, or you can choose to be depressed, hopeless and forlorned by focusing on the negative. The choice is yours.

-
-
-
-
-
-
-

1. On a scale of 1-10, how do you rate yourself on this issue?
2. Why is this important in your life?
3. If you were to improve in this area, how would it affect your life?
4. Who can help you? Perhaps as a role model?
5. What is the first step you will take?
6. When will you begin?
7. Where (on a scale of 1-10) do you want to be a year from now?

PILLAR 15 - KINDNESS

- Being kind does not mean being weak. It's just the opposite in most situations. It can take great strength to be kind when those around you are not even thinking about being kind but would rather be rude and unpleasant.
- It is a lot easier to handle bad news in difficult situations if you can inject kindness into the moment.
- Being kind will diffuse emotionally charged situations.
- Being kind will open doors that are welded shut.
- It costs nothing to be kind.
-
-
-
-
-
-
-

1. On a scale of 1-10, how do you rate yourself on this issue?
2. Why is this important in your life?
3. If you were to improve in this area, how would it affect your life?
4. Who can help you? Perhaps as a role model?
5. What is the first step you will take?
6. When will you begin?
7. Where (on a scale of 1-10) do you want to be a year from now?

PILLAR 16 - LOVE

- Love is perhaps the most misunderstood subject in the world.
- Real love escapes most of us but should be pursued vigorously.
- The Bible says "God is love" — that's the standard. Therefore, we should make a major study of this subject in our lives.
- Love God,

    Love your family,

    Love others,

    Love your work. You will never have to work if you love what you do.

    Love yourself. You cannot give away something that you do not have, so love yourself.

-
-
-
-
-
-

---

1. On a scale of 1-10, how do you rate yourself on this issue?
2. Why is this important in your life?
3. If you were to improve in this area, how would it affect your life?
4. Who can help you? Perhaps as a role model?
5. What is the first step you will take?
6. When will you begin?
7. Where (on a scale of 1-10) do you want to be a year from now?

PILLAR 17 - PATIENCE

- My brother, Doug, tells me there has to be a lot of patience in me because little has come out of me to date.
- Most goals can be achieved with patience and perseverance.
- Being patient does not mean just standing by and waiting.
- You can be persistent without being a patient person. But if you possess both, you will be hard to beat. It is hard to beat someone who is patient and refuses to quit.
-
-
-
-
-
-
-
-
-

1. On a scale of 1-10, how do you rate yourself on this issue?
2. Why is this important in your life?
3. If you were to improve in this area, how would it affect your life?
4. Who can help you? Perhaps as a role model?
5. What is the first step you will take?
6. When will you begin?
7. Where (on a scale of 1-10) do you want to be a year from now?

PILLAR 18 - PEACE

- Harmony with others in your surroundings is extremely valuable and therefore very expensive.
- Peace at any price is not worth the price.
- What would you give for peace
  - in the world?
  - in your neighborhood?
  - with your boss and co-workers?
  - in your marriage?
  - with your family?
  - with yourself?

-

-

-

-

-

-

-

-

1. On a scale of 1-10, how do you rate yourself on this issue?
2. Why is this important in your life?
3. If you were to improve in this area, how would it affect your life?
4. Who can help you? Perhaps as a role model?
5. What is the first step you will take?
6. When will you begin?
7. Where (on a scale of 1-10) do you want to be a year from now?

PILLAR 19 - PROACTIVENESS

- This may not sound like a Pillar, but properly applied it will magnify your other qualities.
- There are times to be silent and wait, and there are times to act.
- It is much easier to steer a moving vehicle. When you "start," all kinds of energy begin to flow — doors open, ideas develop and people show up. Many things will begin to happen that could not have happened until you took action.
- Every journey begins with a single step.
- Take a goal or situation and break it down until you find something you can do now that will propel you to a solution. Take that action and look for the next step. It can be as simple as making a phone call and asking a friend to help you with your situation. Even if they are in no position to help, if they just allow you to verbalize to them, you may be up and running.
- Many people refuse to take any action until they can see how it will all turn out. Usually the result is that nothing happens.
- Number 1 on Steven Covey's list of Seven Habits is to be proactive. This can be just what Covey says – a habit. However, it can work both ways. If you do not become proactive and let that become a habit, then your inaction becomes a habit and that will paralyze your future.
- The intention throughout this book is to focus on the positive. However, many points can be well illustrated by considering the opposite — in this case, procrastination.
-
-
-
-
-

-
-
-
-
-
-
-
-
-
-
-
-

1. On a scale of 1-10, how do you rate yourself on this issue?
2. Why is this important in your life?
3. If you were to improve in this area, how would it affect your life?
4. Who can help you? Perhaps as a role model?
5. What is the first step you will take?
6. When will you begin?
7. Where (on a scale of 1-10) do you want to be a year from now?

PILLAR 20 - RESOLUTION

- It is hard to beat someone who will not quit.
- When a situation demands your best effort and failure is not an option, burn the bridges and make a stand.
- You can always adjust, but never give up.
-
-
-
-
-
-
-
-
-

1. On a scale of 1-10, how do you rate yourself on this issue?
2. Why is this important in your life?
3. If you were to improve in this area, how would it affect your life?
4. Who can help you? Perhaps as a role model?
5. What is the first step you will take?
6. When will you begin?
7. Where (on a scale of 1-10) do you want to be a year from now?

PILLAR 21 – RESPONSIBILITY (PERSONAL)

- Taking responsibility is a rare commodity.
- We all look for ways to avoid responsibility at some level.
- It is much more productive to take responsibility than to blame others.
- Look around – there are endless situations where people did not take any responsibility and are now frantically looking for someone to blame or sue.
- You can pass it off to someone else, but like a boomerang, it will be right back.
- Seeking responsibility is a very good way to get ahead in the world at any level.
- We tend to want to be responsible only for what turns out well.
- The more quickly you take full responsibility for what happens to you, the quicker your life will improve.
-
-
-
-
-

---

1. On a scale of 1-10, how do you rate yourself on this issue?
2. Why is this important in your life?
3. If you were to improve in this area, how would it affect your life?
4. Who can help you? Perhaps as a role model?
5. What is the first step you will take?
6. When will you begin?
7. Where (on a scale of 1-10) do you want to be a year from now?

PILLAR 22 - SERVICE

- Service to others is a major reason we are here.
- This can include giving money, but only giving money to a cause will come up short in creating fulfillment in your life. We can all pray for a person and/or a situation which may be the very best and/or the only thing we can do.
- There is a saying "whatever you are short on, give it away, and it will come right back to you several times over." How this works is beyond my understanding, but it works, i.e., giving your time will create more time in your life.
-
-
-
-
-
-
-
-

1. On a scale of 1-10, how do you rate yourself on this issue?
2. Why is this important in your life?
3. If you were to improve in this area, how would it affect your life?
4. Who can help you? Perhaps as a role model?
5. What is the first step you will take?
6. When will you begin?
7. Where (on a scale of 1-10) do you want to be a year from now?

PILLAR 23 – SILENCE

- Being silent is not a sign of weakness.
- Without silence, music is one long note.
- Being with someone and being silent can be very helpful in difficult circumstances.
- You do not have to take back what you did not say.
- The song says, "Silence is Golden." How true that is. Many times being totally silent is what is needed.

-
-
-
-
-
-
-
-

1. On a scale of 1-10, how do you rate yourself on this issue?
2. Why is this important in your life?
3. If you were to improve in this area, how would it affect your life?
4. Who can help you? Perhaps as a role model?
5. What is the first step you will take?
6. When will you begin?
7. Where (on a scale of 1-10) do you want to be a year from now?

PILLAR 24 - TOLERANCE

- Everyone needs a break from time to time.
- If in doubt, give the other person some space.
- It may be easier to tolerate pain than to tolerate someone you see as different.
- Learning from others is easier if you will first tolerate them being different.
- Tolerance does not mean you should allow yourself to be pushed around or taken advantage of.
-
-
-
-
-
-
-
-

1. On a scale of 1-10, how do you rate yourself on this issue?
2. Why is this important in your life?
3. If you were to improve in this area, how would it affect your life?
4. Who can help you? Perhaps as a role model?
5. What is the first step you will take?
6. When will you begin?
7. Where (on a scale of 1-10) do you want to be a year from now?

- At the bottom of it all – at the foundation of it all – WISDOM.
- The Book of Proverbs. Just read it.
- Enough said!
-
-
-
-
-
-
-
-
-
-
-

1. On a scale of 1-10, how do you rate yourself on this issue?
2. Why is this important in your life?
3. If you were to improve in this area, how would it affect your life?
4. Who can help you? Perhaps as a role model?
5. What is the first step you will take?
6. When will you begin?
7. Where (on a scale of 1-10) do you want to be a year from now?

CHAPTER 5

Priorities

Trying to explain and convince you of what your priorities in life should be is very intimidating for me. They are a bedrock part of this book and as such cannot be ignored. The only approach that will work for me is to stick tight to explaining what works for me. Remember, we are uniquely different and please do not be offended if my explanation of priorities comes up short for your life.

Over the years, the subject of priorities has appeared and reappeared in different packages with a variety of explanations. They clearly depend on the person doing the packaging and explaining. Their individual style and what they have personally experienced has to come out, and it always does.

About 20 years ago, the package I call "The Five F's" crossed my path. My recollection tells me it came from Jim Rohn. In any case, he gets the credit. This grouping is the most concise and all-encompassing of the many to cross my path. What are they?

1. *FAITH*
2. *FAMILY*
3. *FRIENDS*
4. *FITNESS*
5. *FINANCIAL*

There are two main reasons the five F's work for me. First, they are easy to remember and therefore easy to pass on to others. Secondly, every important aspect of my life can find a home under this multi-faceted umbrella.

In considering this particular grouping, it is impossible for me to exclude any of the five F's and still believe a well-directed, balanced and focused life will result from my efforts.

Before analyzing each area, it is important to understand that taken as a whole, none of the areas can or should interfere with any of the other areas. If there is conflict, then something is wrong with the definition or the implementation being used. At first glance, they can appear to be impossible to ever satisfy. My suggestion is that you study and meditate on this list of priorities at length and in great depth. If, in fact, the listing doesn't work for you, by all means adjust. Please let me know what you come up with, as I am open to any improvement you have to offer.

Properly described and understood, your priorities should never change. Goals, subjects to study, and even your personal mission can be adjusted or dropped. I don't believe you can eliminate any of the five F's, and hope to have a satisfying life. Ignoring any of these areas can and will be devastating. You can only sustain a level in your life as high as your weakest point. Let's take a look at the separate priorities.

1. Faith

As the years begin to overwhelm my efforts to secure the fountain of youth, I shudder to think where my life would be leading if my faith was weak or non-existent. In this case, by faith, I mean my relationship with my Creator. As far back as my youth, this was clearly a priority for me. Then, my life was very unsettled and constantly put me at odds with the other four areas that are now also priorities for me. It took a long time and a lot of difficult experiences to shake out. As the fog cleared and my life took better form, it was gratifying to understand that while my faith is of utmost importance, a good understanding of faith means there is not and should not be conflict with the other priorities in my life. This could easily be another book, which most likely I will never write.

Think carefully before you decide this area of your life does not warrant being a priority. When everything is going well, it is easy to let this slide. When your world turns upside down, it is nearly impossible to right without dealing with this neglected priority, if in fact you were neglecting the priority of faith.

2. Family

Growing up with dozens of aunts, uncles and cousins, and three brothers to go along with loving and caring parents and one set of grandparents, made it easy to take family for granted. As the years went by, it became apparent not everyone had this advantage in life.

It is clear to me, but please study this for yourself, that the word "Elohim," most often translated "God" in the Bible, refers not to an individual but to a Family. It is not important or appropriate for me to elaborate on this; however, a careful study of this one idea could very well change your life.

The more diverse your family, the more complex it will become; the more benefits and opportunities, the more challenges and disappointments. Don't fret over this, but rather celebrate!

Just to focus on my relationship with my three brothers for a moment, I am reminded that of the four basic personality types, my parents had the foresight to populate all four. No wonder the four of us have struggled over the years. My relationship with one of my brothers has peaked and now settled into a more separate and more mature situation. With another, we have finally realized we are not the same and it is okay to be that way. With the third brother, we never really had a chance to be close, and I am finally at ease with such a fate.

Our dear Mother put up with a lot of grief from the four of us as we grew up. Fortunately, we now have the opportunity to reward her efforts. Dad had a big hand in how we now relate to Mom. He had a way of letting me know he was depending on me to look out for her after he was gone. I am sure my three brothers got the same message. It is gratifying to have the experience of a very large and diverse family. As I watch "the lights go out" in front of me, it is very rewarding to see new flames emerge as my children start their own families. They will continue to improve and expand on what is already in motion.

Why include all this personal information? Because real family is always personal. I don't know any other way to get the point across. For my life to make sense, family MUST be one of my priorities. Work hard to have, maintain, nurture and trust a good solid family structure. Working hard for your family is really not work.

3. Friends

The word "friend" is like the word "love," both overused. What we need are several words to more clearly define any discussion regarding friends. Actually, there are other words; we just don't use them appropriately. Without going into detail, I'll try to be clear on this subject.

Is it true a friend can be closer than a brother? Absolutely! How can that be? Primarily because you don't get to choose your family. It is also easier to walk away from a friend if the baggage becomes too heavy. The relationship can still remain but at a different level.

So what is the ultimate type of friend? A good friend of mine who lives in Wyoming was told by his father that if he had five real friends, he was a lucky person. He said it took years until he comprehended his father's message. It took me years to be sure five such friends existed in my life. This is how I would define such a friendship. If you found yourself in serious trouble on a cold wintry night and really needed help, who would you call? A "top-shelf" friend would be one who would respond by saying "I'm on my way, and by the way, where are you?" in that order. That may be a little dramatic, but you get the picture. Not many of these relationships exist. If you want that kind of friend, make sure you **ARE** that kind of friend. A good friend can carry you when nothing else works.

My life has been blessed with several irreplaceable friends. It has been and will continue to be a real bonus to know that no matter what happens, there is someone to bail me out when I hit bottom. Randy and I have been through a lot and there were times our friendship was severely tested. Why, I am not sure, but the testing only served to strengthen our relationship.

It's probably best not to mention too many friends by name, only because leaving someone out would really bother me.

Strength can be gathered from friendships that on the surface would have no reason to develop. There is no question that being around certain people brings out the best in certain areas of my life. One such friend is the poster boy for self-discipline. He pushes me, without his ever knowing, to be a better person. He is not wealthy, but he lives well and is quite content and self-assured. He is very talented and works hard; however, money is not a primary goal. He reacts and works the same when he is being paid as when he is working for free. How we became good friends is a mystery. The important point is we both benefit.

As I consider past friendships, I am reminded of how my life is constantly affected by crossing paths years ago with one of the world's best friends. Where he is today, I don't know. He may not even be living. However, if he knocked on my door, we would pick up just where we left off—good friends.

Something to keep in mind is that friends at the "super level" never keep score. They are too focused on giving to the relationship to be bothered with keeping score. Of course, to work smoothly, both parties need to be on the same page. Don't focus on how many friends you have. Don't worry too much about who they are or what you do or don't have in common. Focus on being a good friend when and where you can. Let the friendship develop at its own pace.

4. Fitness

Aren't we really talking about good health here? Yes, but it doesn't start with "F", so . . . .

You do not need to be told your health should be a priority. We all know that without good health everything else in our lives is diminished and necessarily takes a back seat until your health is restored.

The basics are well-known, but oh how we dread the implementation. This should not be the case. The price of good health is worth every demand it places on you. It is easy to find extensive quality information on the benefits of good health and how it can be acquired and maintained. Do you want to lose weight? It's simple [there's that word again]—eat less and exercise more. As usual, the hard part is in the doing. If it was easy, I would not be on a diet at this moment. If dieting was easy . . . well, it just isn't.

Don't beat yourself up on this issue. If you fail, start over. If you fail again, start over again. They don't grant good health as a reward for quitting. Don't feel like the Lone Ranger—you are not the only person who battles this issue.

Keep working on good health. Your mind and body are very forgiving, especially at a young age, but you need to do the basics. Start a better health plan, and start TODAY.

5. Financial

This book is not about making money, but it is in large part about priorities, and finances needs to be one of your priorities. Be sure of this—if you don't make finances a priority, it will become a priority by default at the expense of all the others.

There is a verse in the Bible that says if someone doesn't take care of their family, they are worse than an infidel. As near as I can determine, it was not good to be considered an infidel in Biblical times.

Finances is a very difficult area to keep in balance. There is so much pressure to have more, that we constantly feel we are on a treadmill. Be aware that the people telling you to get more of everything are most likely wanting you to help them get more by buying their product. There is nothing wrong with wanting and striving for more. We are hard wired for more. Madison Avenue and Wall Street supply the software to place all kinds of demands on our lives. Just make sure your money works for you, not against you.

Money is a tricky subject. One of the basics to be aware of is this—whatever you are, money will make you more of it. For example, if you are a generous person when you are making $20,000 a year, you will be even more generous when making $100,000 a year. However, the reverse is also true. People often strive for more money as a cure-all, only to find their situation gets worse when they get the money they sought so vigorously. My prayer is to have more money, but not more than I can handle.

One of the best articles I ever read about finances appeared in the September 23, 2002 issue of the "Wyoming Livestock Round-Up" by Lee Pitts in his column "It's the Pitts." The article, "How to Get Rich," covered five areas —- invest in your community, your home, your marriage, your kids and yourself. He ended with "What's that you say, you don't have the time. My friends, that's all you do have. Invest it wisely."

In this country, a lot of emphasis is placed on making money. When it comes to money management, retention and growth, as a society, we do not do nearly as well.

The financial priority is not all about making money. In the end, how you use what you have is far more important than how much you can acquire.

Conclusion

While the general meaning of all five of these priorities is understood by nearly everyone, it is of the highest urgency that you define these areas for yourself. What is needed is your sustained, concentrated effort to imprint in your mind how very important these priorities are to you and your future.

As you strive to become the person necessary to fulfill your personal mission, never cease to look at life through the lens of priorities. <u>Do your best – this is not a dress rehearsal</u>.

My <u>Priorities</u> in life are:

Notes/Comments

CHAPTER 6

Direction – Balance - Focus

You can expect to get nowhere without working on these three disciplines. Which is the most important? Good question. Which leg of a three-legged stool is most important? The answer is the one that's missing.

Weakness in any of these three areas will have a major impact on future results. If your direction is wrong, the other two are immaterial. Without balance, your progress will be desperately slow. Focus is the rocket fuel that gets you there. Unless your direction and balance are in good order, focus will actually work against you. Your progress will accelerate, but in the wrong direction.

Direction

Number one is going in the right direction. If you are not, everything else becomes meaningless over time. Just as important, you must be GOING. If you want your ship to come in, it needs to be sailing, and it is much easier to steer when it's moving. Be prepared to be off-course most of the time. Don't be alarmed. If you monitor and adjust on a regular basis, you will arrive just fine. A personal mission is critical to set your direction in life. With a lifelong personal mission, you will not have to worry about depression setting in after a major goal is achieved. There will be ups and downs, delays, setbacks and breaks in the action. However, your lifelong personal mission will immediately begin to draw you back into action. If your personal mission is set correctly, there will be no need to continuously motivate yourself. If you are drawn by your personal mission, the motivation will tend to take care of itself.

Where you have been and where you are is not nearly as important as where you are headed.

Balance

Gaining and maintaining good balance in life is a never-ending challenge. It should be viewed as a good thing and not something to get upset about when things turn upside down, as they will from time to time. Most of this book is about balance. All the Building Blocks work best when they are functioning together. You cannot remain effective for long if you pay no attention to areas you find difficult or unpleasant. The old statement, "a chain is only as strong as its weakest link," is very appropriate here. A glaring weakness can destroy everything, i.e., ignoring your health. It may someday be the center of your attention, but to no avail. Many businesses fail because the owner has no interest or ability to deal with one or more of the critical areas necessary for survival of the business. A good businessman will hire others to do what he cannot or would not want to do. When it comes to <u>YOU</u>, life is not that easy. In the final analysis, it is <u>YOU</u> that need the balance in your life. True, you can get a lot of help, and you should, but <u>YOU</u> are the one that needs attention, not your business.

To make reasonable progress, you need balance. All areas of importance must be given proper attention.

Focus

If you have everything in proper balance and know where you are headed, what is so important about focus? As the Building Blocks become more and more a part of your life, it becomes easier to be effective in whatever situation you find yourself. The idea is to string these pieces together so they reinforce each other and become a very strong and dynamic aspect of your life, i.e. controlling your thinking is excellent. By staying relaxed and being positive in all situations, you will begin to master all kinds of situations in which you find yourself.

The idea of "ASK" becomes <u>A</u>sk the right people, <u>S</u>eek in the right place, <u>K</u>nock on the right doors, and do it in a relaxed and positive manner, while you constantly control your thoughts. If you couple this with good health and good appearance . . . , well, you get the picture. If all this works together you will become more and more focused, which enables you to improve and get more balance. Your circle of effectiveness becomes larger, which brings on more situations that require more growth. You will become stronger and more capable as you develop in all these areas.

Unfortunately, the reverse is also true. You will become weaker and less capable if you do not work on these important areas. Life will not allow you to stand still. Sadly, many people are content to "stand still" only to discover later in life that they drifted into a situation they did not want and are now unable to change.

"Probably the most important talent you can have is focus, concentrate and try to do the best you can at what you are trying to do, and do that consistently." Dr. Bob Rotella, world-renowned sports psychologist.

Notes/Comments:

CHAPTER 7

Subjects to Study [STS]

1.	Common Sense	12.	Language
2.	Communication	13.	Leadership
3.	Competition	14.	Marketing
4.	Courage	15.	Music/Art
5.	Current Events	16.	Negotiation
6.	Decision Making	17.	Numbers
7.	Dreambuilding	18.	Philosophy
8.	Failure	19.	Politics
9.	Genealogy	20.	Problem Solving
10.	Goal Setting	21.	Religion
11.	Humor	22.	Retirement

23.   Science/Nature

Astronomy	Northern Lights
Butterflies	Oceanography
Chemistry	Precious Metals
Dogs	Queen bees
Elephants, Eagles, Elk	Reptiles
Fish, Flowers	Salmon
Geography	Trees
Horses	Uranium
Insects	Volcanoes
Jewelry	Weather
Kangaroos	X-rays
Lions	Yeast
Mountain Climbing	Zoos

24.	Self Esteem	28.	Teamwork
25.	Sports	29.	Time Management
26.	Stress	30.	Thinking
27.	Stuff "stuffitis"		

The Subjects to Study are intended to be a starter list for you. Feel free to add and subtract at your pleasure. These areas will help you improve yourself, i.e., goal-setting, decision-making, stress management, and to make your life more interesting, thereby making you more fun to be around as you study subjects such as science/nature, music/art and genealogy.

You do not have to be an expert in a lot of areas but avoid becoming one-dimensional. Robert Kiyosaki says "know a little about a lot." Beware of trying to impress others by trying to convince them you know more than you do. You just need to know enough to ask good questions. When you tap into an area of interest, all you need to do is listen. The other party will be delighted to teach you.

As you continue to research and learn about these STS, you will become much more interesting and better informed in all kinds of areas. Your self-confidence will grow, and others will be happy to be around you. Do not make the mistake of zeroing in on one area and dominating the conversation. Very few people will have your level of interest in whatever the subject is that you have chosen.

For starters, spend an evening on the Internet researching the 26 topics listed under science/nature. You will soon know more in this area than most people you meet.

STS 1 – COMMON SENSE

He has no common sense! That lady has a lot of common sense! How many times have you heard one or the other?

- Everyone wants to know what it is.
- Where does common sense come from? Does anyone know?
- How can you obtain common sense?
- We have all heard people described as well-educated but having no common sense.
- We all want others to have common sense. We should also desire it in ourselves.
- Try this for a definition: the ability to take what you have learned from a wide variety of places and experiences and distill it into usable form when you encounter challenges in new areas.

While running our lumber mill a few years back, we always liked to have employees who had grown up on a farm. These people had a wide variety of experiences and learned to become very resourceful in fixing things and solving problems. Not only were they good workers, but they also had a lot of common sense.

-
-
-
-

1. Why is this STS of interest to you?
2. On a scale of 1-10, what is your level of ability and understanding?
3. Who do you know that could aid you in your research?
4. How do you expect to benefit by spending time and energy on this STS?
5. What, if anything, will you do?
6. When will you start?
7. Where will you be able to use this effectively?

STS 2 – COMMUNICATION

There are various types of communications and each one plays a vital role. From my point of view, speaking, listening, writing and body language are the "big four" and will give you plenty to do for at least one lifetime.

- Fifteen percent of our success depends on and flows from our technical knowledge. Eighty-five percent depends on our ability to interact and get along with other people. You need both, but dealing effectively with others is where it's at in making steady progress.
- Make good use of the reams of excellent material that is readily available on this vital subject.
-
-
-
-
-
-
-
-

1. Why is this STS of interest to you?
2. On a scale of 1-10, what is your level of ability and understanding?
3. Who do you know that could aid you in your research?
4. How do you expect to benefit by spending time and energy on this STS?
5. What, if anything, will you do?
6. When will you start?
7. Where will you be able to use this effectively?

STS 3 – COMPETITION

Whether you enjoy competition or detest its existence, you will find it everywhere you go. A good understanding of competition should not make it appear as "butting heads."

- Business refers to the marketplace as competitors.
- We compete for grades in school, the corner office, the next promotion, a good spot in the parking lot, status, and hundreds of other desired results.
- Sports are all about competition.
- My past has included too much competition, and I do not look for it in any form. Plenty of competition still finds me. The point to consider is <u>the other side of a strong point can be a weak point.</u> In my case, in the area of sports, my competitive spirit served me very well. But it was not so readily appreciated in other areas of my life, and because of that, I had to learn to tone it down.
- An effective level of competition is very positive in various areas of our lives.
- We all benefit from an economy that thrives on competition.
- Study the subject in other people.
- Strive to see how others view you on this point.
- Balance is key. Uncontrolled competition can damage your image beyond repair. You must be capable of translating what you experience in your life into an appropriate and effective level of competition that will work for you, not against you.
-
-
-
-
-
-
-

-
-
-
-
-
-
-
-
-
-
-
-
-
-

1. Why is this STS of interest to you?
2. On a scale of 1-10, what is your level of ability and understanding?
3. Who do you know that could aid you in your research?
4. How do you expect to benefit by spending time and energy on this STS?
5. What, if anything, will you do?
6. When will you start?
7. Where will you be able to use this effectively?

STS 4 – COURAGE

- Putting your finger on a good definition for courage is not an easy task. One that works well for me: the ability to continue despite being unsure and fearful about the outcome. Webster does a really good job on this subject. Look it up.
- Being brave and having courage does not mean you are never afraid.
- You do not have to storm "pork chop hill" to demonstrate you have courage. It takes a lot of courage to stand up to the schoolyard bully.
- Knowingly setting yourself apart from what everyone else is doing requires more courage than most people can muster.
- Many books have been written about individuals on the subject of courage. Why not do some research and reading on Lincoln, John F. Kennedy and Churchill?
-
-
-
-
-
-

1. Why is this STS of interest to you?
2. On a scale of 1-10, what is your level of ability and understanding?
3. Who do you know that could aid you in your research?
4. How do you expect to benefit by spending time and energy on this STS?
5. What, if anything, will you do?
6. When will you start?
7. Where will you be able to use this effectively?

STS 5 – CURRENT EVENTS

Current events are just that -- events that are current. Everyday a wide variety of events take place that affect you and the people all around you. Some events will be major to some people and minor to others. Each day they will ebb and flow. Some are predictable and others are not. Stay up-to-date on what is going on in your community, in your state, across the country and around the world.

There is no need to try to be an expert or watch TV all evening. Just read and observe the daily flow of activity of life around you. People will notice your attention and interest and enjoy talking with you. Try to keep any sharp opinions on your part "off the table."

-
-
-
-
-
-
-
-

1. Why is this STS of interest to you?
2. On a scale of 1-10, what is your level of ability and understanding?
3. Who do you know that could aid you in your research?
4. How do you expect to benefit by spending time and energy on this STS?
5. What, if anything, will you do?
6. When will you start?
7. Where will you be able to use this effectively?

STS 6 – DECISION MAKING

You have probably heard the story about the donkey that starved to death while standing between two piles of hay because he could not decide which one to eat first. Most people will not experience quite that much trouble with decision-making.

Be sure to study this subject along with STS 20 regarding problem-solving. They are too closely-linked to treat separately and too different to consolidate into one issue.

We, as human beings, have the wonderful power of choice. Sometimes the choices are easy, but often they are not. Like it or not, everyday we make choices/decisions even if we believe we have side-stepped them.

As you strive to improve your ability with decision-making, consider these factors:

- Give only small amounts of time and effort to minor decisions. The type of toothpaste you use does not deserve a lot of time and effort. Allocate more time and effort as the decisions get bigger. Bigger here means the size of the impact it will have on your life or on the life of others now and in the future. When confronted with a decision to be made, it is very easy to spend inappropriate amounts of time on the subject. Why that happens is a mystery, at least to me. Perhaps it occurs because the impact of small decisions is not hard to undo and/or will not have a material affect on our lives. Therefore, it is more comfortable to consider the options. Basically, we tend to gravitate to what is easy.

- Understand there are normally only a few factors that really matter to make a quality decision. When buying a cell phone, nobody tears it apart to check out the many details of the unit.

- Look for the fatal flaw. What is the worst that could happen? If you are certain you can manage that result, then there is no fatal flaw. You can go ahead with the decision, confident a bad choice will not wreck your life.

- If you do your homework, sooner or later the decision becomes obvious.

- After making a decision, sleep on it. If it still feels right in the morning, go ahead. My boyhood hero was Davy Crockett.

His motto was "be sure you're right, then go ahead."

A process that has aided me for over 25 years is one I picked up at a seminar in Harrisburg, PA. I would like to give the speaker credit, but I cannot recall his name. Once again, the process is simple. He called it "bootstrapping." It works like this. When confronted with a difficult decision, go back in your mind (or files) and recall a similar circumstance. What was the process you used to make that decision? What exactly did you do? Read material on the subject? Call selected people? And so forth. It does not matter what the process was, only that you can clearly identify what you did.

Several years ago, I was facing a very sticky negotiating dilemma. I was able to recall the process used in resolving over 20 previous situations that turned out favorably. That renewed my spirit and confidence. The process was identified and worked once again.

Consider this side note that is paramount to all of us. It is absolutely vital that children are required to make choices. They can then learn to consider the options, make decisions and experience the results, good or bad. Not requiring children to learn this vital process when the stakes are low leaves them highly vulnerable when the stakes are high. Making a choice off the fast food menu is not going to change their lives. Deciding to try drugs with a friend at age 14 could very well have a drastic effect on their future.

The decisions you make and the actions you take will create your future, your character and your reputation. Consider them carefully.

•

1. Why is this STS of interest to you?
2. On a scale of 1-10, what is your level of ability and understanding?
3. Who do you know that could aid you in your research?
4. How do you expect to benefit by spending time and energy on this STS?
5. What, if anything, will you do?
6. When will you start?
7. Where will you be able to use this effectively?

STS 7 – DREAM BUILDING

Your mind is an amazing piece of high-tech gear. You can achieve what you can conceive and believe. Only a few things can hold you back, which would include:

- Your self-esteem.
- How you use your mind. See Link 1.

How quickly you can achieve your dreams depends on many things:

- Take time to consider and imagine what could become reality in your life. i.e. Nicer home, more vacations, college education, etc.
- Get good at brain-storming.
- Capture your dreams on paper which can then be used as fuel for goal-setting.
- Keep pen and paper handy at all times, including at night. When you get awake with what appears to be a good idea, write it down, in the dark if necessary. Just capture it! You can expand later or discard it if it does not prove to be valuable.

Remember, dream-building is not goal-setting; however, it is a precursor to useful and effective goal-setting.

-
-
-

1. Why is this STS of interest to you?
2. On a scale of 1-10, what is your level of ability and understanding?
3. Who do you know that could aid you in your research?
4. How do you expect to benefit by spending time and energy on this STS?
5. What, if anything, will you do?
6. When will you start?
7. Where will you be able to use this effectively?

STS 8 – FAILURE

Many years ago while working for the Commonwealth of Pennsylvania, it was my good fortune to work for a very fine gentleman by the name of Lew. We had a very good relationship which granted me experience invaluable for running my business soon thereafter. An unforgettable lesson learned at that time concerned the subject of failure. Something went wrong—I don't remember what—but my dissatisfaction was evident. After allowing me to complain about the "failure" for a while, Lew cut me off and said "there's no such thing as failure. You have clearly identified a way that does not work." Now, those may not be his exact words, but it was certainly the exact message. After discussing it for a while, my understanding was forever changed for the better.

Keep these points in mind when you are feeling you have failed:

- Edison failed over 10,000 times on his way to inventing the light bulb. You can be glad he did not get discouraged about failing.
- Failure means this is one way that does not work—try again!
- Real failure is doing the same thing over and over and expecting different results.
- "Fail" your way to success.
- Everyone fails. Anyone saying they don't is really failing BIG TIME.

The main point to remember is one of definition. How do you define failure?

-

1. Why is this STS of interest to you?
2. On a scale of 1-10, what is your level of ability and understanding?
3. Who do you know that could aid you in your research?
4. How do you expect to benefit by spending time and energy on this STS?
5. What, if anything, will you do?
6. When will you start?
7. Where will you be able to use this effectively?

STS 9 – GENEALOGY

What a beautiful subject. My interest here did not take root until later in life. Much to my dismay, many opportunities were missed.

The more you understand about your genealogy, the easier it becomes to understand and appreciate your life and circumstances. There was a time in my life when I could not understand why people would get so caught up because they did not know where they came from and who their ancestors were. Now I understand much better, and my heart goes out to anyone dealing with these issues.

Right around the time my Dad passed away, my interest in our family genealogy began to blossom. There was a lot of information available my entire life, but my interest was too low to take advantage. For several decades, and it continues, there has been a reunion each year for the descendents of Joel Meiser. He was my great grandfather. Unfortunately, I never met him or my grandfather Meiser. After Dad was gone, I decided to pick up the slack because he was always active in the reunion and never missed attending. As we were preparing to attend one year, my son, a teenager at the time, asked if he could go along. Suddenly, it was clear what a poor job I had done in passing along vital family history. My son has been the President of the association for several years and will probably continue as long as he wishes, since the pool of candidates is not very large.

In 2003, in a single moment, Nathan changed his life, and the life of others, by crossing paths with a cousin ten times removed while on a trip to Germany. To illustrate how eventful that has become, consider that cousin Uwe ended up being the best man in Nathan's wedding two years later. Needless to say, they have a super relationship that has benefited our entire family. A book could be written about what all has happened-- hopefully Nathan will do just that in the future.

-

-

-

-
-
-
-
-
-
-
-
-
-
-
-

1. Why is this STS of interest to you?
2. On a scale of 1-10, what is your level of ability and understanding?
3. Who do you know that could aid you in your research?
4. How do you expect to benefit by spending time and energy on this STS?
5. What, if anything, will you do?
6. When will you start?
7. Where will you be able to use this effectively?

STS 10 – GOAL SETTING

Goals are previews of coming attractions. They can be very simple or very elaborate. However you approach goal-setting, there are a number of important points to keep in mind:

- Decide what it is you want. Where do you want to go? What do you want to do? Who do you want to meet? . . . In any case, begin with the end in mind.
- Generate ideas by brain-storming and feeding off your dream-building ideas.
- Write it down. Write it down! WRITE IT DOWN! Did I mention you should write it down? This simple but easily overlooked part of goal-setting will have a dramatic impact on your results.
- Be specific. The more details the better. Clearly define and continue to refine as you go. Wanting more money will not work. Wanting $100 more per month by the end of the year will work.
- One of the essentials – you need a strong reason or reasons, the more the better, why you really need to achieve each goal.
- If you do all the things mentioned so far, you will accomplish many of your goals even if you forget what they are because your subconscious mind will not forget. Recently my son told me he went over a list of goals he had prepared years ago, and he was amazed how many he had achieved, even some he had forgotten were on the list. Your subconscious mind will work 24/7 to accomplish whatever you ask it to do—good or bad. Be careful what you wish for. You just might get it. Poor Judas.
- Anchor your goals with a deadline.
- Do not fret if they sound silly or impossible.
- Write them on 3 x 5 cards and keep them with you. Review them when you have dead spots in your day, i.e. sitting in the dental office waiting area.
- Have goals for all areas of your life.
- Goals in all areas should be congruent and support your personal mission.

- You need goals short-term, long-term and everywhere in between.
- Goals should be out-of-reach, but not out-of-sight.
- With a big goal, start by breaking it down until you have something you can do today that will aid the accomplishment of that goal. An analogy would be taking a trip in a car. You only need to get started—you can work out the turns and detours as you go.
- To be successful with goals and other areas of your life, learn to do what you do not like to do. To be successful in any area of your life, you need to do things you would really rather not have to do. This is a major hurdle or stumbling block for many. The plan is good and everything is set and moves forward. When unpleasant things need to be resolved that can be avoided, the plan fails for lack of commitment and/or the ability to do what needs to be done. The project heads south and is quickly replaced with an even "better" idea which will soon meet the same fate.
- Be flexible. The goal is supposed to serve you, not you serving the goal. It is quite acceptable to abandon a goal.
- If you get discouraged, set a short and very achievable goal, then celebrate your success.
- Review STS 20 regarding problem-solving and STS 6 regarding decision-making.
- "The greatest value of achieving a goal is what you become." – Jim Rohn. One of my goals is to meet Jim Rohn. Perhaps if I had a better reason, I would be successful.
- Excellent books and tapes are plentiful and easy to find on goal-setting.

As you can readily see, this is one of my favorite subjects. I would like to end this STS with several personal experiences concerning a variety of approaches to goal-setting and achievement.

First, <u>flexible goal-setting</u>. During his junior year in high school, my son, Nathan, approached me about what he wanted to do in the future—that was to fly fighter jets for the Air Force. His mother nearly stopped breathing. In any event, we spent a year plus doing everything imaginable attempting to get him admitted to the Air Force Academy. He was not admitted, but what he ended up doing in order to improve his position was to go to Valley Forge Military College (VFMC) for a year to prep. We found this was a very acceptable and often-used approach. While he was there, and before he even started, the Army approached him about joining its ROTC program. The ROTC ended up offering him a full ride at VFMC. Nathan went to Fort Knox that summer to check it out, came home and turned the Army down. While he was at Fort Knox, Nathan became friends with a young man who suggested he should fly for the Navy. His advice was that in order to do that, Nathan should get into one of five different schools that had excellent Naval ROTC programs. So while Nathan was at VFMC, we spent a lot of time applying and eventually getting him admitted to his top choices. His Number 1 choice was Penn State. He transferred to Penn State with a great deal of difficulty because Penn State just did not accept students as sophomores at University Park. He went to summer school at Penn State, went that fall, took several Naval courses, and now 2½ years later, Nathan came home and announced during the holidays that he did not want to do that anymore. That was over 8 years ago, and we have never talked about it since.

Was all that a waste of time? No. The value of the journey was worth a fortune. Incidentally, his mother is breathing again.

The second one – <u>rigid goal-setting</u>. My youngest daughter, Kathy, was looking to get a degree in music industry. That degree is not offered by many schools. So we were looking around, trying to figure out the best place to go, or I should say, "a" place to go.

Upon arriving home from a hunting trip in Montana, I discovered that Kathy had zeroed in on James Madison University (JMU) in Virginia. We figured her acceptance there would be a slam-dunk because she had done so well in high school. When we went down to visit, we found out that was not the case. The music school there is very small, and they recruit for those spots about the same way they recruit for the football team. We were amazed and realized we had a lot of work to do. First off, her mother and I suggested she might want to apply to a few other schools. "Now why would I do that, Dad?" "Well, just in case." "Just in case what?" "In case you don't get accepted here." "Why wouldn't I get accepted?" "I don't know, but you might not. Perhaps you should apply to a couple other schools." "But I want to go to JMU." "All right, let's give it all we got." She was accepted and graduated right on time, with honors.

Third one – <u>routine goal-setting</u>. Our oldest daughter, Leslie, did well in high school. She picked out the subject she wanted to major in, selected the geographical area she wanted to be in, and picked five schools. She checked them out, visiting two of the schools, and then selected Albright College in Reading, PA. Leslie went to Albright and graduated with honors. It was almost like there weren't any goals. But there were goals, and lots of them.

Fourth one – <u>The 24 Hour Special</u>. Visiting my favorite haberdashery, I discovered a beautiful leather jacket that I desperately wanted but was unable to justify within my budget. When it went on sale, I really got wound up. After some additional consideration, I decided if the money could be created—new money, not existing or expected—before someone else purchased the jacket, it would be mine. Less than 24 hours later, it was mine.

Fifth one – <u>Almost There</u>! I have been drooling over a ranch in Wyoming for a long time. A picture of the ranch hangs in my office. The purchase is complete except for two things. Everything else is set and ready to go. Those two details? First, it's not for sale, and secondly, I don't have the money.

The ranch is a constant stream of enjoyment. Sometimes I think it is more pleasure for me than it is for the current owners. My theory is at some point the ranch will be for sale, and someone will be the new owner. Why not me?

-

-

-

-

-

-

-

-

-

-

-

-

-

-

-

-

-

-

1. Why is this STS of interest to you?
2. On a scale of 1-10, what is your level of ability and understanding?
3. Who do you know that could aid you in your research?
4. How do you expect to benefit by spending time and energy on this STS?
5. What, if anything, will you do?
6. When will you start?
7. Where will you be able to use this effectively?

STS 11- HUMOR

How do you react to humor? Does it often seem out of place? Much of life is about balance, and so it is with humor. Solomon says there is a time to laugh and a time to cry. Be sure to get it right.

It is a documented fact that we learn better and quicker when humor is part of the equation.

People have told me to never insert a joke in a serious conversation, and others have advised me to lighten up a tense situation with a little humor. So what's the answer? My suggestion is to study the subject, especially by watching people you and others respect. Consider these ideas:

- Properly handled, humor can take the stress out of most—not ALL—situations.
- We are the only creatures on earth that can laugh—there must be a good reason.
- God laughs.
- You can get away with saying almost anything if you wrap it in humor. As always, your heart must be in the right place.

Don't try to change your personality, but you can surely adjust the dial on how effective you are in using humor. Be prepared with a comeback if you "bomb," as we all do. Put it on yourself, not the other person.

Humor helps us learn, relieve stress and makes life more enjoyable. The teachers I remember best are the ones that had a good balance of discipline and humor. People will respond to the humor, and thereby limit the need for much discipline. Christ said "Be more like a child," and we all know that children love to laugh and play. Humor will always make life more enjoyable, with or without the trappings of success.

Think about it. Would you rather work on a project you believe will be fun, or one without any fun in site?

-

-

-

-
-
-
-
-
-
-
-
-
-
-
-
-

1. Why is this STS of interest to you?
2. On a scale of 1-10, what is your level of ability and understanding?
3. Who do you know that could aid you in your research?
4. How do you expect to benefit by spending time and energy on this STS?
5. What, if anything, will you do?
6. When will you start?
7. Where will you be able to use this effectively?

STS 12 – LANGUAGE

Where would we be without the ability to use language. Language has always been important, especially since the Tower of Babel. At a young age, this subject never impressed me much. Too bad for me. Fortunately, for my age group, it's never too late to start.

Studies show a relationship between vocabulary and crime. Being unable to express themselves verbally, a person often resorts to a less appropriate means of expression. Vocabulary is vital. Work on it everyday.

Over the years, my work has placed me around the Amish community. What a delight to see how easily their children pick up a second language. If you have a gift for foreign languages, use it. If not, work extra hard on your native tongue.

-
-
-
-
-
-
-

1. Why is this STS of interest to you?
2. On a scale of 1-10, what is your level of ability and understanding?
3. Who do you know that could aid you in your research?
4. How do you expect to benefit by spending time and energy on this STS?
5. What, if anything, will you do?
6. When will you start?
7. Where will you be able to use this effectively?

STS 13 – LEADERSHIP

Are great leaders made or born? According to Rudolph Giuliani, they can be made. This is a favorite subject of mine, but I will keep my remarks brief and encourage you to research and study leadership with a passion. Several points to start your thinking:

- We are all required to be leaders at some level.
- If you aspire to be a leader, understand you may not be very popular, at least not in the early stages.
- Many skills are required to be an effective leader. Fortunately, most of them can be learned.
- Mountains of good material exist on leadership. One of the best books on the subject, in my opinion, is the book <u>Leadership</u> by Rudolph W. Giuliani. Don't miss this one. Keep it handy and re-read when you have a leadership challenge.
- Do not confuse leadership with control. Control is an addictive substance and will not elevate you as a leader.
- No. 1 – Remember – you will not be able to do it all yourself. Trying to is not leadership.
- Great leaders have great vision, accept blame and dispense credit.
- This subject is a never-ending quest. You never stop becoming a leader; you are always pursuing the art of leadership.
-
-

1. Why is this STS of interest to you?
2. On a scale of 1-10, what is your level of ability and understanding?
3. Who do you know that could aid you in your research?
4. How do you expect to benefit by spending time and energy on this STS?
5. What, if anything, will you do?
6. When will you start?
7. Where will you be able to use this effectively?

STS 14 – MARKETING

My education in this area really started when my oldest daughter, Leslie, majored in business marketing at Albright College. When my son, Nathan, also received a business marketing degree at Penn State, I was hooked.

We are not talking about sales here. Mention marketing and/or sales, and most people will be turned off. Their position is they do not like sales. Like it or not, we are all in the business of marketing every day of our lives.

- The Madison Avenue approach may turn you off, but be sure they know what they are doing.
- Address this as something to be enjoyed and valued as basic to your future well-being.
- Read the book <u>The One to One Future</u> by Don Peppers and Martha Rogers, PhD. The book is basically about business, but we are all in the business of marketing ourselves.
-
-
-
-
-

1. Why is this STS of interest to you?
2. On a scale of 1-10, what is your level of ability and understanding?
3. Who do you know that could aid you in your research?
4. How do you expect to benefit by spending time and energy on this STS?
5. What, if anything, will you do?
6. When will you start?
7. Where will you be able to use this effectively?

STS 15 – MUSIC/ART

My Father would say, "there must be a lot of music in me because none ever came out." In my case, it seems to have passed nicely to the next generation.

My youngest daughter, Kathy, has a Music Industry degree from James Madison University. My interest in music grew as she did, and it was a very enjoyable time in my life. Most of the people around me most likely do not realize that music is something very enjoyable to me. Although my abilities are short in music, as with art, that does not mean my interest is short. A friend of mine, an artist, once told me, "Buy what you like and you'll never be sorry with the purchase." What he was trying to say was don't buy it as an investment. In both art and music, I know what I like.

Music is all around you. Take a few minutes each day to tap in and enjoy good music. Pick one area and focus on it for a period of time. There is no need to be an expert to enjoy and share interests. Music people really light up when you show interest and give them permission to talk.

"Music is the mind of God resonating through 10-dimensional hyper-space." Professor M. Kaku.

-
-
-
-

1. Why is this STS of interest to you?
2. On a scale of 1-10, what is your level of ability and understanding?
3. Who do you know that could aid you in your research?
4. How do you expect to benefit by spending time and energy on this STS?
5. What, if anything, will you do?
6. When will you start?
7. Where will you be able to use this effectively?

STS 16 – NEGOTIATION

So you do not like this subject? Perhaps you should, since you negotiate all the time whether you realize it or not. The quality of your life depends, in large part, on how well you negotiate.

Negotiating does not necessarily mean compromise. Compromise gets a bad rap because many see it as a sign of weakness. While it may well be part of negotiating, compromise does not define negotiating. Use the process to find something of greater value for both parties.

The key to effective negotiation is to find out what the other party wants and then help them achieve their goal. Zig Zeigler said "help enough other people get what they want, and you will get what you want."

When my confidence is running low, I draw on past negotiating success to get me through difficult situations. Meditate on this for a while and you will discover past successes you forgot about.

-
-
-
-
-
-

1. Why is this STS of interest to you?
2. On a scale of 1-10, what is your level of ability and understanding?
3. Who do you know that could aid you in your research?
4. How do you expect to benefit by spending time and energy on this STS?
5. What, if anything, will you do?
6. When will you start?
7. Where will you be able to use this effectively?

STS 17 – NUMBERS

Being a CPA, I am doomed to have a constant parade of numbers dancing in my head. I do not consider that a negative. It is enjoyable to find ways to reduce most situations to numbers. Do not confuse numbers with money.

There is a wealth of ways to look into this subject. Let me recommend two of them to get you started. One, read the book The 80/20 Principle by Richard Koch. Second, read and study the story of the sower in the Bible.

If you are not a numbers person, you will not find this subject very exciting; however, your efforts will be rewarded.

By the way, do you know how many people you need in a room or anywhere to have a 50/50 chance that two of them will have the same birthday, meaning the same month and day? What are the odds that two people on this earth have the exact same number of hairs on their heads?

-
-
-
-
-
-

1. Why is this STS of interest to you?
2. On a scale of 1-10, what is your level of ability and understanding?
3. Who do you know that could aid you in your research?
4. How do you expect to benefit by spending time and energy on this STS?
5. What, if anything, will you do?
6. When will you start?
7. Where will you be able to use this effectively?

STS 18 – PHILOSOPHY

Simply stated, your philosophy is the set of beliefs that govern your life. That being said, it should be apparent that a clear understanding of your philosophy is imperative for a stable and progressive life. It does not matter if you recognize it or not, it will always be there.

The following is a short list of ideas to consider to get started on a study of this immense and emotional topic:

- Philosophy changes by generation, nationality, race, gender and many other categories.
- Your being different does not make you right or wrong. It just means you are different.
- If your philosophy is taking you in a direction you do not wish to go, it is imperative you challenge your set of beliefs.
- To challenge your belief, you simply need to ask "why do I believe what I believe." Facing up to the answer and making the necessary changes will be the hard part.
- If another person has a belief you cannot understand, you at least have to acknowledge and consider that belief, or there is no way you will ever benefit.
- If you spend all your time trying to justify your current beliefs, then that is what you will do—spend all your time justifying your current beliefs.
- If what you believe on any subject does not make sense, why stick with such a belief?
- You heard the statement, "you have to have faith." True enough, but faith in what? I prefer to have faith in what I know, not what I do not know. Life is a very intense puzzle. You do not have to get it all correct by the time you reach adulthood. Everyone is working on a different puzzle. Therefore, in large part, you have to do it yourself.
- The best discussion I ever came across on philosophy was on a set of tapes, The Art of Exceptional Living, by Jim Rohn, published by Nightingale-Conant. Thanks, Jim. Why not start there?
-
-

-

-

-

-

-

-

-

-

-

-

-

-

1. Why is this STS of interest to you?
2. On a scale of 1-10, what is your level of ability and understanding?
3. Who do you know that could aid you in your research?
4. How do you expect to benefit by spending time and energy on this STS?
5. What, if anything, will you do?
6. When will you start?
7. Where will you be able to use this effectively?

STS 19 – POLITICS

Why in the world would politics be included in this chapter, or anywhere else in this book for that matter? It is understood we should stay away from politics and religion, right? As a general rule, yes. Here's my point. You either need to (1) stay away from politics, or (2) become very good at discussing this subject without offending others.

Politics is a big part of our culture. Therefore, it is wise to be aware of what is going on and understand how it affects you, your community, state, nation and the world we all call home. Learn to ask questions and strive to not overly react regardless of what others say. Many of my friends are not aligned politically with me. We have learned to avoid hitting each other's hot buttons.

-
-
-
-
-
-
-

1. Why is this STS of interest to you?
2. On a scale of 1-10, what is your level of ability and understanding?
3. Who do you know that could aid you in your research?
4. How do you expect to benefit by spending time and energy on this STS?
5. What, if anything, will you do?
6. When will you start?
7. Where will you be able to use this effectively?

STS 20 – PROBLEM SOLVING

Problem-solving has a lot to do with decision-making, but it is not the same. Keep these points in mind when a problem presents itself:

- The best time to attack the problem is as soon as it appears. Problems seldom go away and tend to get bigger.
- It is critical to know when to react and when not to react. If you do not open the door, often it is a smoke screen and not a real problem.
- It may be helpful to replace the word "problem" with the word "challenge," "opportunity" or whatever word will quiet your mind and allow you to think.
- The time to ignore a problem is when it is not yours, and someone wants to make it yours.
- Leadership, management and dealing with people are primarily about problem-solving.
- A bad temper is a real liability when injected into problem-solving.
- Review boot-strapping which is covered in STS 6 – Decision-Making.
- If you are really stuck, start with a blank piece of paper and list at least 20 approaches that could be considered to resolve the situation at hand. Include the extremes.
- Quiet time is very helpful. My attorney likes to kid me that he charges me for "shower time," since he thinks best there and therefore can better solve my legal problems. He is kidding, I hope.

Since I have not been able to completely separate problem-solving and decision-making, I would suggest you read and study both. There is no need to focus on making them separate issues.

-
-
-
-

-
-
-
-
-
-
-
-
-
-
-
-

1. Why is this STS of interest to you?
2. On a scale of 1-10, what is your level of ability and understanding?
3. Who do you know that could aid you in your research?
4. How do you expect to benefit by spending time and energy on this STS?
5. What, if anything, will you do?
6. When will you start?
7. Where will you be able to use this effectively?

STS 21 – RELIGION

SEE THE DISCUSSION ON POLITICS. THE SAME PRINCIPLES APPLY.

There is one more thing to consider. It is my belief we are wired to need a strong anchor in our life regarding religion. We are very threatened when our cherished beliefs are challenged in any way. Be especially sensitive when dealing with other people in this area.

-
-
-
-
-
-
-
-
-

1. Why is this STS of interest to you?
2. On a scale of 1-10, what is your level of ability and understanding?
3. Who do you know that could aid you in your research?
4. How do you expect to benefit by spending time and energy on this STS?
5. What, if anything, will you do?
6. When will you start?
7. Where will you be able to use this effectively?

STS 22 – RETIREMENT

To the best of my knowledge, this word or concept does not appear anywhere in the Bible. In my opinion, that can give us a lot of discretion on the subject. However, we need to think about it seriously. In our society, it is a huge subject, especially in my age group.

Brilliant people exist at all ages, but truly wise people are most often retired or approaching that magic age. What that means to me is while we may well need to retire from our jobs, we should look forward to making contributions to our family, neighborhood, and so forth in different ways. Many people do this. The ones who do not end up not feeling very good about themselves. Jim Rohn says, "Doing less than we can messes with the mind." Not a real elegant way to say it, but he gets the point across. We need to stay busy and contribute or our self-esteem suffers. When that happens at any age, it is not good.

My father retired just before I started my business. He chipped in and helped me a great deal. A few years later he told me he was glad I started a business because all his retirement plans had been completed the first year of his retirement.

What does retirement mean to you? Make sure you have a plan regarding what you will do after you leave your career position.

-
-
-

1. Why is this STS of interest to you?
2. On a scale of 1-10, what is your level of ability and understanding?
3. Who do you know that could aid you in your research?
4. How do you expect to benefit by spending time and energy on this STS?
5. What, if anything, will you do?
6. When will you start?
7. Where will you be able to use this effectively?

STS 23 – SCIENCE/NATURE

What a vast and rich subject. A list of 30 STS could easily be compiled without going beyond this area. Just for fun, why not start with the following A to Z list. A short study in these areas will open up volumes of opportunity to expand your interest and knowledge. Here's the list with some very brief comments:

Astronomy – the advances in astronomy in the past 50 years are mind-boggling.

Butterflies – start with Monarchs, they are absolutely fascinating.

Chemistry – chemistry will introduce you to the building blocks of the universe.

Dogs – if you don't have one, I'll bet one of your neighbors does.

Elephants, Eagles, Elk – take your pick; they are all winners.

Fish/Flowers – I couldn't decide which one to leave out.

Geography – do you know where the Falkland Islands are located?

Horses – they may be more popular now than before cars made the scene.

Insects – most are not that appealing, but a very big pool of subjects. If this isn't your "bag," try Icebergs.

Jewelry – bound to interest you or your spouse.

Kangaroos – these cute fellows will open up all of Australia.

Lions – king of the beasts and a great introduction to cats.

Mountain climbing – a mountain climber I met at the Denver Airport introduced me to a fascinating book, Into Thin Air, by Jon Krakauer. Unfortunately, I never even got the man's name.

Northern Lights – what a show!

Oceanography – oceans cover three-fourths of the earth's surface. Science is just getting started in this "deep" subject.

Precious metals – it is hard not to get excited about gold and silver. Do you know where white gold comes from?

Queen Bees – unbelievable; I just couldn't leave them out of the list.

Reptiles – not one of my favorite subjects, but many people are very fond of this vast and amazing group.

Salmon – just where do they go? I don't know but I do understand how they find their way home.

Trees – having made a living in the forest products industry for many years, like my father, uncles, grandfather, brother and son, I can assure you this super subject will reward your research efforts.

Uranium – do you know how this element affects world peace?

Volcanoes – an unbelievable event that nature uses to amaze us and reshape the earth.

Weather – very safe subject. It is out of our hands and everyone knows that, so we can all safely complain. Most of us are unable to hold a five minute conversation without resorting to the weather.

X-rays – not so long ago, the discovery of x-rays by William Roentgen in 1895 changed the medical profession forever.

Yeast – a lowly subject that we all benefit from.

Zoos – spend an unforgettable day at one near you.

-
-
-
-
-

1. Why is this STS of interest to you?
2. On a scale of 1-10, what is your level of ability and understanding?
3. Who do you know that could aid you in your research?
4. How do you expect to benefit by spending time and energy on this STS?
5. What, if anything, will you do?
6. When will you start?
7. Where will you be able to use this effectively?

STS 24 – SELF-ESTEEM

This is not a subject to be taken lightly. My background does not enable me to be of much assistance to you regarding self-esteem. My hope is you will (1) take this seriously and study the subject; it will not be hard to find material—the hard part will be in making the changes; (2) consider this list that has been helpful to me:

- If you think you can or think you cannot, either way you are right.
- For whatever reason, we can rarely rise above the limit we place on ourselves. You need to change the limit, or you will be right back where you started very quickly.
- Believe in yourself; challenge yourself.
- Love your neighbor as yourself. This does not mean you should be haughty, brag and be pushy. It just means like yourself and feel optimistic about your future.
- Take this seriously if you want to move ahead.
- A simple way to improve your self-esteem – say thank you when someone gives you a compliment.
-
-
-
-
-

---

1. Why is this STS of interest to you?
2. On a scale of 1-10, what is your level of ability and understanding?
3. Who do you know that could aid you in your research?
4. How do you expect to benefit by spending time and energy on this STS?
5. What, if anything, will you do?
6. When will you start?
7. Where will you be able to use this effectively?

STS 25 – SPORTS

True, not everyone is interested in sports, but it is a good guess you know a lot of people who are interested.

It is not hard to know a little about sports because they exist everywhere. So many types of sports exist that you can most likely find one of interest. Most of the time you only have to listen and smile to show interest. My enthusiasm has waned regarding sports, but just mention the Los Angeles Dodgers, actually I prefer the Brooklyn Dodgers, Penn State football, the Duke Blue Devils or the Boston Celtics, and watch my excitement return.

My interest in sports as a young person really needed to be tempered. The problem was I confused interest in sports with competition. Yes, sports involve all kinds of competition, but you can side-step the intense competition while having a valid and avid interest in sports.

Make sure you have fun with sports. If you do not, skip it and go to another subject of more interest. According to my friend, Capt. Edward A. Davis, USN Retired (Vietnam POW August 1965 – January 1973), "If you're not having fun, you're not doing it right."

-
-
-
-

1. Why is this STS of interest to you?
2. On a scale of 1-10, what is your level of ability and understanding?
3. Who do you know that could aid you in your research?
4. How do you expect to benefit by spending time and energy on this STS?
5. What, if anything, will you do?
6. When will you start?
7. Where will you be able to use this effectively?

STS 26 – STRESS

Too much stress can kill you. Having no stress means you are already dead. Obviously, we need a little balance here.

Stress will bring out the best or worst in us, depending upon the subject and situation. Too much stress can make all kinds of things worse, especially heart-related issues. We need to manage it appropriately.

There is a never-ending supply of good material to aid you in managing stress. Make it part of your library and routine. Allow me to offer one piece of advice regarding a routine that helps me. Develop a method to relax in the midst of a crisis. Find a way to access a quiet, peaceful place in your mind. A place you can go to quickly and at will. I love Wyoming and can go there (in my mind) in a flash.

-
-
-
-
-
-
-

1. Why is this STS of interest to you?
2. On a scale of 1-10, what is your level of ability and understanding?
3. Who do you know that could aid you in your research?
4. How do you expect to benefit by spending time and energy on this STS?
5. What, if anything, will you do?
6. When will you start?
7. Where will you be able to use this effectively?

STS 27 – STUFF "stuffitis"

Stuff and the lack of value therein:

- Stuff is supposed to serve us, not the other way around.
- When so much stuff exists in your life that you cannot keep track of what you have, you have too much.
- Our family recently moved. Fortunately, it was not to a small house. What a nightmare! We discovered all kinds of stuff we did not know we had. The shock was so great, not only to me but my wife and children as well, that it has changed our buying habits. We even went on a family vacation instead of buying more stuff for each other at Christmas. The other aftershock was to create the word "stuffitis" and put it in my list of STS.
- Stuff has become a major frustration to a lot of people. Don't become afflicted with "stuffitis."
-
-
-
-
-
-

1. Why is this STS of interest to you?
2. On a scale of 1-10, what is your level of ability and understanding?
3. Who do you know that could aid you in your research?
4. How do you expect to benefit by spending time and energy on this STS?
5. What, if anything, will you do?
6. When will you start?
7. Where will you be able to use this effectively?

STS 28 – TEAMWORK

- Whether you are a follower or a leader, you need to understand the dynamics involved in good teamwork.
- Teamwork can and will span many areas of your life. Chances are slim that you will never be involved with teamwork.
- On the lighter side, boring chores can be fun if you team up with your spouse, a friend or a co-worker.
- You do not always need to be the leader. Find out what it is like to fill various roles in different projects.
- Make an honest attempt to learn from each person you work with on every project that comes along.
-
-
-
-
-
-
-

1. Why is this STS of interest to you?
2. On a scale of 1-10, what is your level of ability and understanding?
3. Who do you know that could aid you in your research?
4. How do you expect to benefit by spending time and energy on this STS?
5. What, if anything, will you do?
6. When will you start?
7. Where will you be able to use this effectively?

STS 29 – TIME MANAGEMENT

The study of time management can be general or very detailed. The 80/20 rule applies here as well as anywhere. You can make great strides quickly in time management. A few pointers:

- If you do not have a Day-Timer or the equivalent, get one and use it everyday.
- Let your Day-Timer do the remembering so you can do more important things.
- If you are stuck on a problem, jot it down a few days hence. Your subconscious can work on the solution and your Day-Timer will bring it to your attention at the appropriate time.
- The amount of material and information available on time management is never-ending. It all basically revolves around the same issues. However, each one will have a different slant and offer unique pieces of useful techniques. Get started and expect great results.
- Consider these facts regarding your time – nobody has more than you do; you cannot create time, only manage it; whenever it's gone, it's gone forever.
- Don't forget that the object is to manage your time so you are more productive and have less stress, as opposed to spending most of your time trying to manage your time.
-
-
-

1. Why is this STS of interest to you?
2. On a scale of 1-10, what is your level of ability and understanding?
3. Who do you know that could aid you in your research?
4. How do you expect to benefit by spending time and energy on this STS?
5. What, if anything, will you do?
6. When will you start?
7. Where will you be able to use this effectively?

STS 30 – THINKING

A while back I purchased a set of videos from The Teaching Company on the subject, "The Joy of Thinking" by Professors Edward B. Burger and Michael Starbird. It turned out not to be at all what I had in mind, but the videos did make me think. The basic theme was to present thinking as a subject to be studied, mastered and enjoyed. Albert Schweitzer was asked one time, "What is wrong with men today?" His answer, "they just don't think." Here are the 10 main points from the video:

1. Make mistakes and learn.
2. Never give up.
3. Keep an open mind.
4. Explore the consequences of new ideas.
5. Seek the essentials. (Don't get side-tracked with a lot of side shows.)
6. Understand the issue.
7. Understand simple things deeply. (As you can imagine, I like the word simple. Don't gloss over something that seems simple. Make sure you really understand the subject matter, rather than just saying "yeah yeah.")
8. Break a difficult problem into a series of simpler, smaller ones.
9. Examine issues from several points of view.
10. Look for patterns and similarities.

This is a great set of videos, one you should take seriously. Yes, anyone can think. Anyone can play baseball too, but some are better players than others. It is that way with thinking. If you think about the right things and use the correct process, it will work out to your benefit.

-
-
-
-
-

-

-

-

-

-

-

-

-

-

-

-

-

1. Why is this STS of interest to you?
2. On a scale of 1-10, what is your level of ability and understanding?
3. Who do you know that could aid you in your research?
4. How do you expect to benefit by spending time and energy on this STS?
5. What, if anything, will you do?
6. When will you start?
7. Where will you be able to use this effectively?

CHAPTER 8

Links – A Yardstick to Live By

Unleashing The Power of Your Mind

1. Control What You Think About

2. Relax and Stay That Way Under Pressure

3. Be Positive

Health & Physical Appearance

4. Maintain Good Health

5. Maintain a Good Appearance

6. Structure Your Environment to Speak of Success

Reacting to Life

7. Be Quick to Admit Your Mistakes, and Quick to Forgive Others for Their Mistakes

8. Control Your Temper

9. Control Your Language

10. Be Happy and Productive

11. Enjoy Every Moment

12. Happiness is the Way

Using Time

13. Make Good Use of Your Time

14. What You Can Dream – Begin

15. Know When to Wait and Be Quiet

16. Spend Time Alone Each Day

Dealing With Others

17. Do Unto Others as You Would Have Them Do Unto You

18. Do Unto Others as They Would Have You Do Unto Them

19. Be a Good Listener

20. Be Nice to People

21. Smile and be Pleasant to Others

22. Be Interested in Others

23. Avoid Negative People

24. Avoid Win-Lose Situations

25. Like Yourself

Moving Ahead

26. Ask and it Shall Be Given
    Seek and You Will Find
    Knock and it Will Be Opened unto You

27. Steady Effort Brings Prosperity; Hasty Speculation Brings on Poverty

28. Counsel With Others on Important Matters

29. Seek Value

30. Be an Educated Risk Taker

31. Be a Decision Maker – Choose!

Getting Things Done Successfully

32. Develop and Maintain Self-Confidence and Self-Control

33. Be Responsible

34. Do It Now!

35. Never Give Up – Never, Never Give Up!

36. I Can Do All Things Through Christ Who Gives Me Strength

The Links are the means by which you put everything into play. All the other Building Blocks are there to provide a solid foundation and structure to aid effective use of the Links in pursuit of your personal mission.

Properly understood and implemented, there will be no conflict among the Links or with the other Building Blocks. There is no need to do them all at the same time. Start where you are. Stick with the ones you are good at, while you strive to improve in weak areas. As you come to the end of each Link, be sure to rate yourself. Be honest. This is for your eyes only. NOTE: If you add or subtract from the 36 Links, it will not be a yardstick to live by. I guess you could add three and call it a "meter to live by" — suit yourself.

NOTE: There is some repetition in the Links (regarding other Building Blocks). Each area is to stand alone and therefore some comments need to be repeated.

LINK 1 – CONTROL WHAT YOU THINK ABOUT

- This is Number 1 for a reason. Numbers 2 through 36 are not in descending order of importance. It would not make sense to me to try to place them in such an order. However, #1 is #1.

- If you get control of what you are thinking about implemented in your life, life becomes a lot easier.

- If you do not get a good handle on your thinking, you will constantly fight through the roadblocks created by not controlling what goes on between your ears.

- Any serious presentations I have read or heard regarding improving life have always covered this subject. It is an area that nearly everyone agrees is important.

- There is no need to "reinvent the wheel" here. With a little effort, you can find volumes of good information on the subject.

- This point truly fits the subject of this book – Simple – Hard – But Simple.

- If you think you can or think you cannot, either way you are correct.

- What you think determines how you feel, and how you feel determines how you act – so be careful what you think.

-

-

-

---

1. On a scale of 1-10, how do you rate yourself?
2. What can you do to increase your ability with this Link?
3. Who can help you?
4. Where will you begin?
5. Why do you consider this important?
6. Where do you want to be on a scale of 1-10 in 30 days, and in one year?

LINK 2 – RELAX AND STAY THAT WAY UNDER PRESSURE

- A good friend of mine was CEO of a large company in the Harrisburg, PA area. At dinner one evening, around the time of his retirement, I asked him this question – What is the most important thing you have learned during your tenure as CEO. He thought for a while, and then said "Relax – 90% of my decisions didn't really matter."
- New York City and the entire country can be glad Rudolph Guliani remained calm on September 11, 2001.
- If you can relax, you will think more clearly.
- Some people seem to be able to rise to the occasion in emergency situations and contribute greatly, while others are paralyzed and unable to do much of anything.
- Use anger only in a very controlled situation.
- You can practice this by remaining calm in minor situations that will help produce positive results. Then, when life blindsides you with a difficult situation, you will be ready.
-
-
-
-
-

1. On a scale of 1-10, how do you rate yourself?
2. What can you do to increase your ability with this Link?
3. Who can help you?
4. Where will you begin?
5. Why do you consider this important?
6. Where do you want to be on a scale of 1-10 in 30 days, and in one year?

LINK 3 – BE POSITIVE

- It's your choice – the only person you can hope to control is yourself.
- Keep your thoughts positive because they control your life.
- <u>Affirmation</u> - I keep my thoughts positive, because they control my life.
- People are about as happy as they make up their minds to be. – Abraham Lincoln.
-
-
-
-
-
-
-
-
-

1. On a scale of 1-10, how do you rate yourself?
2. What can you do to increase your ability with this Link?
3. Who can help you?
4. Where will you begin?
5. Why do you consider this important?
6. Where do you want to be on a scale of 1-10 in 30 days, and in one year?

LINK 4 – MAINTAIN GOOD HEALTH

- Exercise, eat well and get adequate rest.
- Fitness is a must (one of the five priorities – see Chapter 5).
- Your body is your #1 vehicle.
- Consider the "what if" – what if you didn't have good health?
- Maintenance is a lot easier than a major repair.
- The problem is – what is easy to do tends to be easy not to do. This is true here and in many other aspects of life.
-
-
-
-
-
-
-
-
-

1. On a scale of 1-10, how do you rate yourself?
2. What can you do to increase your ability with this Link?
3. Who can help you?
4. Where will you begin?
5. Why do you consider this important?
6. Where do you want to be on a scale of 1-10 in 30 days, and in one year?

LINK 5 – MAINTAIN A GOOD APPEARANCE

- People should not judge you by your appearance—guess what? They do!
- You will feel better about yourself. It affects everything you do.
- Better overdressed than underdressed.
- Find someone you can rely on for good advice in this area.
- We are not talking only about clothing.
- You don't want people to remember what you wore, just that you were well-dressed.
- Present yourself well. You only get one chance to make a first impression.
-
-
-
-
-
-
-
-

1. On a scale of 1-10, how do you rate yourself?
2. What can you do to increase your ability with this Link?
3. Who can help you?
4. Where will you begin?
5. Why do you consider this important?
6. Where do you want to be on a scale of 1-10 in 30 days, and in one year?

LINK 6 – STRUCTURE YOUR ENVIRONMENT TO SPEAK OF SUCCESS

- The people you associate with will have a huge affect regarding how you are perceived.
- This is important in all areas of your life, not just with whom you associate.
- Don't overdo it, but build your surroundings carefully.
- Moderation in all things.
- People are attracted to successful people.
- Make a list of all the areas in your life where this is important. Then determine where you are with each one and how you can improve.

-
-
-
-
-
-
-
-

1. On a scale of 1-10, how do you rate yourself?
2. What can you do to increase your ability with this Link?
3. Who can help you?
4. Where will you begin?
5. Why do you consider this important?
6. Where do you want to be on a scale of 1-10 in 30 days, and in one year?

LINK 7 – BE QUICK TO ADMIT YOUR MISTAKES, AND QUICK TO FORGIVE OTHERS FOR THEIR MISTAKES

- Defending yourself unnecessarily takes a lot of time and energy. Nobody is right all the time, although our egos want us to think we are. Does the situation really matter?
- It makes it easier for others to forgive you.
- Pick your fights carefully.
-
-
-
-
-
-
-
-
-
-
-

1. On a scale of 1-10, how do you rate yourself?
2. What can you do to increase your ability with this Link?
3. Who can help you?
4. Where will you begin?
5. Why do you consider this important?
6. Where do you want to be on a scale of 1-10 in 30 days, and in one year?

LINK 8 – CONTROL YOUR TEMPER

- When you lose control of your temper, you lose control of other areas—what you say, etc.
- People will back away from you if you cannot control your temper.
- Positive does not flow from a hot temper.
-
-
-
-
-
-
-
-
-
-

1. On a scale of 1-10, how do you rate yourself?
2. What can you do to increase your ability with this Link?
3. Who can help you?
4. Where will you begin?
5. Why do you consider this important?
6. Where do you want to be on a scale of 1-10 in 30 days, and in one year?

LINK 9 – CONTROL YOUR LANGUAGE

- What you say and how you say it.
- Language is one of the major tools to effective communications.
- You cannot take back what you say.
- "Sticks and stones . . . but words don't . . ." – yes they do!
- Work on your vocabulary everyday. It is much easier that way.
-
-
-
-
-
-
-
-
-

1. On a scale of 1-10, how do you rate yourself?
2. What can you do to increase your ability with this Link?
3. Who can help you?
4. Where will you begin?
5. Why do you consider this important?
6. Where do you want to be on a scale of 1-10 in 30 days, and in one year?

LINK 10 – BE HAPPY AND PRODUCTIVE

- One feeds the other. Unproductive people are generally not very happy and vice-versa.
- All the money in the world cannot buy happiness. However, all the happiness in the world cannot buy money either. They really don't have much to do with each other.
- Focus in this area and life will be easier and more fun.
-
-
-
-
-
-
-
-
-
-

1. On a scale of 1-10, how do you rate yourself?
2. What can you do to increase your ability with this Link?
3. Who can help you?
4. Where will you begin?
5. Why do you consider this important?
6. Where do you want to be on a scale of 1-10 in 30 days, and in one year?

LINK 11 – ENJOY EVERY MOMENT

- This very moment is the most precious slice of time you will ever have.
- What else is there?
- It is a matter of positive mental attitude and focus.
- Learn from the past, but don't live there. Prepare for the future, but don't get ahead of yourself. Focus on the moment and use it wisely.

-
-
-
-
-
-
-
-
-

1. On a scale of 1-10, how do you rate yourself?
2. What can you do to increase your ability with this Link?
3. Who can help you?
4. Where will you begin?
5. Why do you consider this important?
6. Where do you want to be on a scale of 1-10 in 30 days, and in one year?

LINK 12 – HAPPINESS IS THE WAY

- Learn to be content and happy with what you have and where you are, while pursuing what you want. Learn to enjoy the journey, not just the destination.
- If you cannot find happiness during the journey, you definitely will not find it at your destination.
- Most people are happier when working towards a goal then when they actually achieve it.
-
-
-
-
-
-
-
-
-

1. On a scale of 1-10, how do you rate yourself?
2. What can you do to increase your ability with this Link?
3. Who can help you?
4. Where will you begin?
5. Why do you consider this important?
6. Where do you want to be on a scale of 1-10 in 30 days, and in one year?

- Understand the value of five minutes (Napoleon).
- Be organized and be prepared to use your time well when opportunities present themselves in blocks of unexpected time.
- You have no guarantee of tomorrow.
- Life comes at you fast and steady. What you do with each day affects everything that comes later.
- Time is the great equalizer.
- You can recycle lots of things, but not wasted time.
-
-
-
-
-
-
-
-

1. On a scale of 1-10, how do you rate yourself?
2. What can you do to increase your ability with this Link?
3. Who can help you?
4. Where will you begin?
5. Why do you consider this important?
6. Where do you want to be on a scale of 1-10 in 30 days, and in one year?

LINK 14 – WHAT YOU CAN DREAM – BEGIN

- Boldness has power, magic and genius in it – "Famous" Amos.
- When there is no vision, the people perish - Proverbs 29:18
- It is much easier to steer a moving vehicle.
- Dream big. It's better to shoot for the moon and miss than to aim at nothing and hit dead center.

-
-
-
-
-
-
-
-
-
-
-

1. On a scale of 1-10, how do you rate yourself?
2. What can you do to increase your ability with this Link?
3. Who can help you?
4. Where will you begin?
5. Why do you consider this important?
6. Where do you want to be on a scale of 1-10 in 30 days, and in one year?

LINK 15 - KNOW WHEN TO WAIT AND BE QUIET

- Psalm 46:10 – "Be still and know that I am God."
- Music with no pauses is just noise.
- It is part of the process. You will get more done in the long run.
- Some people find it very difficult to take a break and will continue to work while you try to talk with them. I've seldom seen a good working relationship develop from such a habit.
- Pushing yourself too hard can become a very destructive habit. You need to stop and "sharpen your saw" on occasions.
- Doing nothing can be a good thing unless, of course, it's overdone.
-
-
-
-
-
-
-
-

---

1. On a scale of 1-10, how do you rate yourself?
2. What can you do to increase your ability with this Link?
3. Who can help you?
4. Where will you begin?
5. Why do you consider this important?
6. Where do you want to be on a scale of 1-10 in 30 days, and in one year?

LINK 16 – SPEND TIME ALONE EACH DAY

- Learn to enjoy being by yourself. In the final analysis, we have to go it alone. We can have and should have a support team, but we are responsible for our own outcome.
- You will never really be alone because God will never leave you.
- Spending time alone can become a very effective habit.
- Spending 30+ minutes doing nothing and being alone may be one of the most difficult things you will ever do.
-
-
-
-
-
-
-
-
-

1. On a scale of 1-10, how do you rate yourself?
2. What can you do to increase your ability with this Link?
3. Who can help you?
4. Where will you begin?
5. Why do you consider this important?
6. Where do you want to be on a scale of 1-10 in 30 days, and in one year?

LINK 17 – DO UNTO OTHERS AS YOU WOULD HAVE THEM DO UNTO YOU

- Golden Rule. Sounds like it should work just fine. Matthew 7:12; Luke 6:31.
- When you don't know what to do, this is the best approach.
- This really should not need a lot of explanation.
-
-
-
-
-
-
-
-
-

---

1. On a scale of 1-10, how do you rate yourself?
2. What can you do to increase your ability with this Link?
3. Who can help you?
4. Where will you begin?
5. Why do you consider this important?
6. Where do you want to be on a scale of 1-10 in 30 days, and in one year?

LINK 18 – DO UNTO OTHERS AS THEY WOULD HAVE YOU DO UNTO THEM

- Think about it.
- Other people don't always want what you want.
- If you already know, or can find out, what they want, you can then use this approach to everyone's advantage.
- Direct descendant of Link 17.
- This is often referred to as the "Platinum Rule."

-

-

-

-

-

-

-

-

-

1. On a scale of 1-10, how do you rate yourself?
2. What can you do to increase your ability with this Link?
3. Who can help you?
4. Where will you begin?
5. Why do you consider this important?
6. Where do you want to be on a scale of 1-10 in 30 days, and in one year?

LINK 19 – BE A GOOD LISTENER

- Perhaps the most overlooked aspect of good communications.
- Everyone wants to be heard.
- It must be important because it's not easy.
- Hearing is not listening.
-

-

-

-

-

-

-

-

-

-

-

1. On a scale of 1-10, how do you rate yourself?
2. What can you do to increase your ability with this Link?
3. Who can help you?
4. Where will you begin?
5. Why do you consider this important?
6. Where do you want to be on a scale of 1-10 in 30 days, and in one year?

LINK 20 – BE NICE TO PEOPLE

- Surely everyone wants this in return.
- There is no penalty for being nice.
- Being nice never goes out of style.
- Be polite and show respect.
- Will cost you nothing and can yield high returns.
-
-
-
-
-
-
-
-
-

1. On a scale of 1-10, how do you rate yourself?
2. What can you do to increase your ability with this Link?
3. Who can help you?
4. Where will you begin?
5. Why do you consider this important?
6. Where do you want to be on a scale of 1-10 in 30 days, and in one year?

LINK 21 – SMILE AND BE PLEASANT TO OTHERS

- The international language.
- You can get away with a lot and/or soften the blow if you smile; i.e. if you have difficult news to deliver, it will be easier for the other person to accept and deal with if you relax and smile.
- Smiling requires less energy than frowning.
- It will make people wonder what you're up to.
-
-
-
-
-
-
-
-
-
-

---

1. On a scale of 1-10, how do you rate yourself?
2. What can you do to increase your ability with this Link?
3. Who can help you?
4. Where will you begin?
5. Why do you consider this important?
6. Where do you want to be on a scale of 1-10 in 30 days, and in one year?

LINK 22 – BE INTERESTED IN OTHERS

- Better to ask questions and listen than talk about yourself.
- MMFI – Make Me (others) Feel Important and treat others as if MMFI were stamped on their forehead.
- People will tell you a lot if they know you are interested in them.
- Others don't care what you know until they know you care.
-
-
-
-
-
-
-
-
-
-

1. On a scale of 1-10, how do you rate yourself?
2. What can you do to increase your ability with this Link?
3. Who can help you?
4. Where will you begin?
5. Why do you consider this important?
6. Where do you want to be on a scale of 1-10 in 30 days, and in one year?

LINK 23 – AVOID NEGATIVE PEOPLE

- Life is too short to waste time with negative people.
- Negativity breeds negativity.
- You simply cannot afford to spend time with these people.
- Don't walk – RUN – from negative people.
-
-
-
-
-
-
-
-
-
-
-

1. On a scale of 1-10, how do you rate yourself?
2. What can you do to increase your ability with this Link?
3. Who can help you?
4. Where will you begin?
5. Why do you consider this important?
6. Where do you want to be on a scale of 1-10 in 30 days, and in one year?

LINK 24 – AVOID WIN-LOSE SITUATIONS

- Seek win-win or no deal.
- Also avoid lose-win and lose-lose situations and people. Yes, there are people who would rather lose than allow you to win (gain).
- Help others get what they want and you will get what you want - Zig Ziglar.
- Finding out what others want can be difficult, especially when they don't know what they want either.
- If you create a win for yourself at a loss for the other person, they will not be there for you the next time.
-
-
-
-
-
-
-
-
-

1. On a scale of 1-10, how do you rate yourself?
2. What can you do to increase your ability with this Link?
3. Who can help you?
4. Where will you begin?
5. Why do you consider this important?
6. Where do you want to be on a scale of 1-10 in 30 days, and in one year?

LINK 25 – LIKE YOURSELF

- Love your neighbor as yourself.
- You might be the only one. "I'm not much, but I'm all I think about." - Anonymous
-
-
-
-
-
-
-
-
-
-
-

1. On a scale of 1-10, how do you rate yourself?
2. What can you do to increase your ability with this Link?
3. Who can help you?
4. Where will you begin?
5. Why do you consider this important?
6. Where do you want to be on a scale of 1-10 in 30 days, and in one year?

LINK 26 – ASK AND IT SHALL BE GIVEN

Seek And You Will Find
Knock And It Will be Opened

- Ask the right people.
- Seek in the right places.
- Knock on the right doors.
- Do your research.
-
-
-
-
-
-
-
-
-

1. On a scale of 1-10, how do you rate yourself?
2. What can you do to increase your ability with this Link?
3. Who can help you?
4. Where will you begin?
5. Why do you consider this important?
6. Where do you want to be on a scale of 1-10 in 30 days, and in one year?

LINK 27 – STEADY EFFORT BRINGS PROSPERITY; HASTY SPECULATION BRINGS ON POVERTY

- Check it out – overnight success stories are almost always backed by years of effort.
- "Overnight success" usually takes about 15 years.
- Easy come, easy go is all too often true.
-
-
-
-
-
-
-
-
-

1. On a scale of 1-10, how do you rate yourself?
2. What can you do to increase your ability with this Link?
3. Who can help you?
4. Where will you begin?
5. Why do you consider this important?
6. Where do you want to be on a scale of 1-10 in 30 days, and in one year?

LINK 28 – COUNSEL WITH OTHERS ON IMPORTANT MATTERS

- This is a must if you expect to grow.
- Experience is the best teacher, especially if it's someone else's experience.
- Most people want to and will help you if you give them a chance.
- Wise men learn from the mistakes of others, fools learn from their own.
-
-
-
-
-
-
-
-
-

1. On a scale of 1-10, how do you rate yourself?
2. What can you do to increase your ability with this Link?
3. Who can help you?
4. Where will you begin?
5. Why do you consider this important?
6. Where do you want to be on a scale of 1-10 in 30 days, and in one year?

- It does not matter what it costs. The important question is – what is it worth? What a revelation this was to me. If I recall correctly, this was on a Jim Rohn tape. That made all his tapes and material worth the price several times over.
- Don't let the "Yeah Yeah" factor overwhelm you here. Most of us are inclined to look for a "good deal," which generally means cheap.
- Look through the "lens of value," not cost.
- Value is what we're after, unless you're a lose-lose person.
- The pain of poor value will overwhelm the pleasure of a "good deal."
- Walk away as soon as you realize the value is not there. Cut your losses. Donald Trump is credited with being very good at this. Don't be guilty of chasing a "good deal," thereby getting in deeper and deeper.
- The subject of Negotiation (see STS 16) gets real big and very important in this area.
-
-
-
-
-

1. On a scale of 1-10, how do you rate yourself?
2. What can you do to increase your ability with this Link?
3. Who can help you?
4. Where will you begin?
5. Why do you consider this important?
6. Where do you want to be on a scale of 1-10 in 30 days, and in one year?

LINK 30 – BE AN EDUCATED RISK TAKER

- Look for the fatal flaw in what could happen that would deal an unacceptable blow to your life.
- Know the facts of a situation.
- Be prepared.
- Act at the correct time. Timing can be everything.
- Be sure you are right, then go ahead. Davy Crockett (my boyhood hero).
- Know a little about a lot. It's often more helpful than knowing a lot about a little.
- Lifelong education is a must.
- Many people will not get on board until it's a proven success. Which is, of course, too late.
-
-
-
-
-
-
-
-

1. On a scale of 1-10, how do you rate yourself?
2. What can you do to increase your ability with this Link?
3. Who can help you?
4. Where will you begin?
5. Why do you consider this important?
6. Where do you want to be on a scale of 1-10 in 30 days, and in one year?

LINK 31 – BE A DECISION MAKER – CHOOSE!

- Again – look for the fatal flaw.
- Decide and get things moving. Adjust as you go.
- Use "boot strapping" in decision making. (STS 6)
- This will put you ahead of the crowd.
- Your greatest power is your power to choose.
- Works hand in hand with Link 30.
-
-
-
-
-
-
-
-
-
-

1. On a scale of 1-10, how do you rate yourself?
2. What can you do to increase your ability with this Link?
3. Who can help you?
4. Where will you begin?
5. Why do you consider this important?
6. Where do you want to be on a scale of 1-10 in 30 days, and in one year?

LINK 32 – DEVELOP AND MAINTAIN SELF-CONFIDENCE AND SELF CONTROL

- A must to get through difficult situations.
- Pause before you act. I have heard most people in prison would not be there had they done this one simple thing.
- The time between an event and your reaction is vital.
- Keep your head while others are losing theirs.
-
-
-
-
-
-
-
-
-
-

---

1. On a scale of 1-10, how do you rate yourself?
2. What can you do to increase your ability with this Link?
3. Who can help you?
4. Where will you begin?
5. Why do you consider this important?
6. Where do you want to be on a scale of 1-10 in 30 days, and in one year?

LINK 33 – BE RESPONSIBLE

- Take the pressure off others. They will work better and help you more freely.
- It is better and easier than looking for someone to blame.
- Great way to move ahead.
- You will stand out with others because most people simply cannot do this.
- In the end it is YOUR life and it is YOUR responsibility.
-
-
-
-
-
-
-
-
-

1. On a scale of 1-10, how do you rate yourself?
2. What can you do to increase your ability with this Link?
3. Who can help you?
4. Where will you begin?
5. Why do you consider this important?
6. Where do you want to be on a scale of 1-10 in 30 days, and in one year?

LINK 34 – DO IT NOW!

- Do it!
- As Nike says, Just do it!
- Begin. Adjust as you go.
- Be proactive.
- If it can be done in two minutes, do it now rather than put it on the "to do" list.
- Procrastinators never get anything done.
-
-
-
-
-
-
-
-
-

1. On a scale of 1-10, how do you rate yourself?
2. What can you do to increase your ability with this Link?
3. Who can help you?
4. Where will you begin?
5. Why do you consider this important?
6. Where do you want to be on a scale of 1-10 in 30 days, and in one year?

LINK 35 – NEVER GIVE UP!

- "Never give up – never, never give up!" - Churchill.
- It may be appropriate to change direction and/or goals, but don't give up on the priorities of your life.
- See Chapter 9 regarding quitting.
- Persistence/perseverance will take you a long way in life.
-
-
-
-
-
-
-
-
-
-

1. On a scale of 1-10, how do you rate yourself?
2. What can you do to increase your ability with this Link?
3. Who can help you?
4. Where will you begin?
5. Why do you consider this important?
6. Where do you want to be on a scale of 1-10 in 30 days, and in one year?

LINK 36 – I CAN DO ALL THINGS THROUGH CHRIST WHO GIVES ME STRENGTH

- You can do it with Christ's help. He will never leave you.
- If God is for us, who can be against us?
-
-
-
-
-
-
-
-
-
-
-

---

1. On a scale of 1-10, how do you rate yourself?
2. What can you do to increase your ability with this Link?
3. Who can help you?
4. Where will you begin?
5. Why do you consider this important?
6. Where do you want to be on a scale of 1-10 in 30 days, and in one year?

Notes/Comments:

Part III

Is This the Beginning or the End?

CHAPTER 9

How to Quit

Anyone making a serious effort to fulfill a well thought out and meaningful personal mission is bound to hit a brick wall on occasion. It is essential to have a strategy in mind to deal with these difficult circumstances. Early on in my life, I had no such strategy. Please feel free to learn from my not being prepared.

Historically, refusing to quit had always been an objective of mine, so quitting was off limits as a subject to consider. However, when everything falls apart and the pressure and stress have reduced you to inaction with absolutely no way out, you really need to know how to quit. Discovering how to do this was not by design, but resulted directly from the previous statement. This may sound like a complete contradiction to everything else this book represents, but I am quite serious.

First, you need to accept the idea of quitting and give yourself permission to do just that. After you review the entire situation and you are convinced it is indeed hopeless, announce to yourself that you are quitting. No ifs, ands or buts, you have made a firm decision to quit. Tomorrow, first thing, you will quit. Not today, but tomorrow! Given that, if you really have given yourself permission to quit, your mind will just shut down and let everything go. By tomorrow, things will change. Perhaps your goal will change, your understanding may adjust, or the importance of the situation just goes away. Regardless of what transpires, you will be able to proceed. Repeat "medication" as often as needed to achieve the desired result. You need to reserve this for serious situations or it can become a useless exercise. Think of it this way – one of your priorities is being threatened, which could drastically upset everything you stand for. In a very difficult case like this, you really need to find answers and strength. This has proven to me to be the only way to get back on track and to be inspired to continue. In a way, perhaps you're just kidding yourself, but when it works, you will be amazed and very glad you "tricked" yourself.

CHAPTER 10

The Key that Always Works

Didn't we just cover that in Chapter 9? Yes and no. Sometimes you have no time to quit because you are in a very time-sensitive situation that will not wait until tomorrow. You need to respond quickly. So what's the answer?

As a Christian, it is clear to me where the power of my life comes from and that problems and difficulties arise for my own good. This concept is at times more than I can accept, but I do believe it's true.

Your faith may be different than mine, and that's okay. I will assume you believe in God. This approach may be more of a solution to problems that you believe have a solution which you are unable to locate at the moment. It can be quite difficult, pressing and upsetting for the moment, but not necessarily going to wreck your life if you cannot deliver as needed. In any case, what has always worked for me is to admit that this is important and I simply do not know what to do. With this in mind, I find a very private spot [no need to be fancy], kneel down and say a very short [about 15 seconds or so] and very specific prayer regarding my immediate needs. After that very short and intense session, I get up and go deal with the situation. Answers come out of nowhere and never cease to amaze me. NOTE: These sessions cannot be used to "get what you want," but rather to accept help when you are in over your head. The answer that arrives may not be the one you were looking for, but it will be the one needed at the moment. There is no doubt in my mind that we are allowed to get into these situations, or perhaps put in these situations, to allow us to develop this very effective skill.

CHAPTER 11

In the End

In the end, everything we have will go to someone else and everything we are goes with us. Part of who we are is what we leave behind – not only things and "stuff," but how we have affected others and how we will affect others after we are gone. The impact of this never hit me until my Father passed away. His influence is greater on me now than when he was living. There is nothing wrong with the accumulation of things and leaving them behind. We are to provide for our grandchildren. That's two generations hence! However, that should not be the major purpose of our lives.

Perhaps the most valuable resource we have to offer others is time. Time is part of your very being. What's the saying, nobody ever inscribed "I wish I'd spent more time in the office" as an epitaph for their tombstone.

In any case, what you leave others in terms of "things" is seldom cared for and appreciated compared to what others earn and create on their own. Who we are goes with us forever. That being the case, surely we would want to give it top billing while we are here on earth.

Human nature, being what it is, allows us to put off what doesn't appear to be urgent at the moment. Meditate each day on the fact that, in the end, what we have become is all we have to take along. What we leave behind may be valuable and benefit many others, but you can't take it with you. Fulfillment of your personal mission has a dramatic impact on (1) what we leave behind; and (2) what you take with you. The most valuable aspect of your personal mission will not be the outcome of the mission, but rather who you have become in the process. Set your personal mission high and never give up!

CHAPTER 12

Success

Having worked your way through this book, you have now outlined sufficient work to occupy the rest of your life. Must you now wait until the very end of your life to determine if you were successful?

If you are going to be successful, you first have to define "success." If you ask 100 people for their definition, chances are good 90 or more would include dollar signs. That is not what we are looking for here. Being successful does not mean you do not have problems. How you deal with and resolve problems will be a measure of success in itself. Success should certainly include an element of pleasure as well.

So what is success? Do not, I repeat DO NOT, let anyone tell you what your definition of success should include. Trying to live up to another's expectations for your life will leave you feeling anything but successful. Where it first appeared, I am not sure, but I know it is included in Earl Nightingale's tape, <u>The Strangest Secret</u>, and it is hands-down the best definition of success ever to come into my life. "<u>Success is the progressive realization of a worthy ideal</u>." If you adopt this definition, you do not need to wait until the end of the year, until your kids are out of school, or much less until the end of your life to feel and celebrate success. The truly beautiful aspect is that you can apply this definition effectively to your personal mission, every single Building Block, and every other area of your life that is important to you. The best part is, you can have and experience success now!

By all means, research and consider many approaches. In any case, make sure you define success in a way that will work for you on a day-to-day basis. Let me repeat my definition of success — "success is the progressive realization of a worthy ideal." Perfect! Each day you can declare yourself a success. Picture it! Each day is wrapped in success. Every morning you can unwrap the gift created yesterday and use the new day to create even more success.

My definition of <u>Success</u> is:

Notes/Comments

CHAPTER 13

Personal Mission Stool

The Personal Mission Stool is a simple visual designed to stay in tune with the rest of this book. It took a while to complete, but in the end it came together very quickly. It is important for you to take some time and create a mental picture of the scene. I have deliberately not included a picture to go with this chapter. The visual needs to be yours and yours alone.

The floor represents the Pillars that provide the foundation for everything else. If the floor is strong and flat, everything will work much better. Obviously, if the floor is weak and uneven, it will not matter very much what kind of stool is placed there.

The Subjects to Study are represented by the surroundings of the furniture in the room, artwork, the view out the window, and whatever else would work with the stool to make it more interesting and useful. Without the surroundings, the stool would be much less interesting. The surroundings could be very specific or very general, but the idea is that you will continually study different areas and continually rearrange this room and look for a better and better setting for the stool.

The Direction, Balance and Focus would work somewhat like this. The Direction would be the use of the stool. We need to know exactly what we are trying to do with the stool, so while it may seem rather simple, without knowing what you are going to do with it, not having the stool in an upright position, you have no direction and the whole thing falls apart.

The Balance of the stool is strongest and solid if all four legs are touching the floor at the same time. That would be unlike some of the chairs in our kitchen. An uneven floor or variation in the length of the legs could be the problem. In other words, if the floor is not solid and level, or if the legs are weak or not fitted together properly into the overall structure, then your balance is out of whack.

The Focus is that the stool is not trying to be something else. It is completely focused on being a stool and serving that purpose.

The Priorities are faith, family, friends, fitness and financial, or the five F's, as I like to call them. The Faith part of the stool would be the seat, because that's the focus of what this stool is all about. The entire structure is there to support the seat. Without the seat, it has no function. The four legs of the stool represent Family, Friends, Fitness and Financial. If one of these is weak or missing, sooner or later the pressure will be on in that area, and everything can go down. So you might get by short-changing your family in order to achieve financial success, but when the pressure is on with the family, everything can come crashing down. You simply cannot ignore any of these areas to have a successful life.

The Links are represented by the rungs on the stool. The more rungs there are, the better they are fitted together and the stronger they are individually, the better and stronger the stool. If the links are poorly developed and not fitted properly, they will not add a lot of value. However, if they are made out of good materials and properly fitted, the more you add, the stronger the whole structure becomes.

So you have the whole structure with the foundation, the surroundings, and the stool itself all there to assist you as you develop and fulfill your personal mission. The better each of these areas is developed, the more useful the stool.

A very plain and otherwise unnoticed stool could become quite elegant and useful if properly crafted, placed in the right setting and used by a person to aid in the accomplishment of a great task. An example might be an artist who does tremendous work using the stool to assist him.

In summary, the idea is to visualize the stool when necessary to aid you in staying focused. For example, let's say you are having a bad day and things are not going well. You simply recall this stool. It will not be hard to remember the pieces and you can just think about, focus and meditate on this stool. Try to see exactly where you are having a problem. Is it in the foundation? Is it in the surroundings? Or is it in the structure itself? This exercise will bring you right back into focus to aid in fulfilling your mission. You need to keep in mind that the entire concept here is that the stool supports your mission.

If you are going to have a worthwhile mission, something that is going to encourage you to grow and be there for you for the rest of your life, it needs to have a solid foundation and a solid structure for support. You cannot fulfill much of a mission if you have your whole life screwed up with all sorts of gaps and weak spots. While the mission will be yours and yours alone, and that is the way it should be in my opinion, we are not put here to be clones of each other, but to be unique individuals. Therefore, we all need the foundation, structure and all the things that need to be developed, none of which will be easy.

The whole concept of this book is that life is simple; hard, but simple. These concepts are not difficult to absorb and not difficult to appreciate or understand, but some of them are just about impossible for me to implement into my life effectively. Everyone will find some of them difficult. To the extent you can develop and implement them into your life, you become much more capable in fulfilling your personal mission.

Your mind works best with pictures. My recommendation would be to develop in detail every aspect of the stool and its surroundings. You can then use this picture of the stool and its surroundings to quickly and easily bring yourself back into focus when necessary.

My personal mission stool:

CHAPTER 14

Have a Great Mission!

Congratulations! You have arrived at the end, or the beginning, depending upon your perspective. If your resistance is running high, do not be concerned. My resistance was so strong it took me over twenty years to complete this project. If this task looks nearly impossible and a lifetime of work, you are correct. It certainly will take the rest of your life.

Taking the CPA exam years ago was an experience not soon forgotten. It was not designed to be completed, at least not by me or anyone else in my circle that took the exam. It was an exercise about what you can get accomplished in two and a half days. It reminds me of the point of the personal mission—what can you get done in a lifetime? Good things take time. Great things tend to happen all at once, but only if you are prepared. Be prepared.

I have shared a lot with you throughout the pages of this book. Since the focus of the book is heavily weighted toward your personal mission, you have a right to expect me to share mine with you. After a lot of consideration, I have decided against doing so. Primarily, because I do not want to influence what you select as your personal mission. My personal mission is rather simple. It contains only nine words. Actually, it could be clearly stated with three words, but that's just _too_ simple.

My friend, if you have not started on your personal mission at this point, why not get started right now? Go out there and make a statement with your life!

"Oh, Terry, you do not understand my circumstances." I am sure I don't, but you are not your circumstances, you are YOU.

"Oh, I don't have time." You have as much as anyone else. You have the rest of your life, and no one has more than that.

"Oh, I'm not very well-educated." Neither was Albert Einstein.

"Oh, I'm not very good-looking." According to whom? I'm not either, and I get by.

"Oh, I don't have much money." It doesn't take money to think. You have to think to have money and hold on to it.

"Oh, all my friends will laugh." So what? I would suggest that they are not really friends if they do.

"Oh, I'm not very smart." Compared to what? You have the most sophisticated piece of gear [computer] in the world right between your ears. Your only rival will be others who are trying like you are.

"Oh, I'm too busy at work." Not too busy to think on the way to and from work, on break or at lunch. Add 20 minutes to your day by getting up 20 minutes earlier. After three weeks, it will be a habit and you will have created three 40-hour weeks every year to work on your mission.

"Oh, there are other reasons." I am sure there are, and none of them will hold you back unless you consent. My friend, make a promise to me and yourself—make a statement with your life!

My intention is to use and adjust this information as long as I live. Beyond that, it is my hope and prayer that now or later, this material will help at least one other person.

Make my day – be the ONE!

Have a Great Mission!

P.S. Not only can you write in this book, but in doing so it will become your book. It will change from being my book into a book about you and your life that you write as you proceed throughout your days on this earth.

APPENDIX I

Biblical Anchors

Introduction

Part I - What Is This All About?
    Chapter 1 - My Guidance System
               Proverbs 10:25
    Chapter 2 - Three Basic Questions of Life
    Chapter 3 - Personal Mission
               Matthew 25:14-30, Romans 12:2+,
               Ephesians 1:11+; Philippians 2:13, and
               Proverbs 16:9

Part II - Building Blocks

    Chapter 4 - Pillars
        1. Appreciation
            I Thessalonians 5:18
        2. Character
            Proverbs 10:9, Ecclesiastes 7:1
        3. Compassion
            Judges 5:9, Matthew 9:36
        4. Contentment
            Romans 9:20, Ecclesiastes 6
        5. Discipline
            Ecclesiastes 7:8, Galatians 5:22+, Proverbs 25:28,
            James 3:13
        6. Faith
            Luke 17:5+
        7. Faithfulness
            Galatians 5:22, Proverbs 25:13
        8. Forgiveness
            Mark 11:25, Psalm 51:17
        9. Frugality
            John 6:12

10. Generosity
   Ecclesiastes 11:1, Proverbs 11:24+, Mark 12:43
11. Honesty
   Psalm 34:12+, Proverbs 3:3 and 12:22, Luke 16:10
12. Humility
   Proverbs 18:12, 22:4, and 29:23, Isaiah 57:15
13. Industry
   Proverbs 6:6+, 10:4-5, 13:11, and 22:29,
   Ecclesiastes 2:10 and 9:10
14. Joy
   Proverbs 3:13+, Galatians 5:22
15. Kindness
   Proverbs 3:3, I Corinthians 16:14, Galatians 5:22
16. Love
   I Corinthians 13, Colossians 3:14, Matthew 22:36-40
17. Patience
   Galatians 5:22, Proverbs 25:15
18. Peace
   Psalm 34:14, Matthew 5:9, Galatians 5:22
19. Proactiveness
   Matthew 25:26+, Acts 24:25
20. Resolution
   Romans 7:23+, Proverbs 21:31
21. Responsibility
   Ecclesiastes 9:10
22. Service
   Matthew 20:28 and 23:11
23. Silence
   Proverbs 10:14, 19
24. Tolerance
   Galatians 5:22
25. Wisdom
   Book of Proverbs

Chapter 5 - Priorities
   Faith
   Hebrews Chapter 11, Matthew 8:13, Mark 9:23,
   Luke 17:5, II Corinthians 5:7, James 2:17,

I John 5:4
Family
Proverbs 22:6
Friends
Ecclesiastes 4:9+, Proverbs 17:17, 18:24,
and 27:10, Romans 12:10
Fitness
Genesis 1:29 and 9:3
Financial
I Timothy 5:8, Ecclesiastes 5:10+
Proverbs 13:22, 13:7, 21:20, 24:3+ and 28:20

Chapter 6 - Direction – Balance – Focus
Direction
Psalm 139:13+
Balance
Ecclesiastes 3:1+
Focus

Chapter 7 - Subjects to Study
I Corinthians 9:22, Proverbs 15:14

1. Common sense
   Proverbs 3:21
2. Communication
   Proverbs 13:17 and 6:12-15
3. Competition
4. Courage
   II Chronicles 17:6
5. Current events
6. Decision-making
7. Dreambuilding
8. Failure
9. Genealogy
10. Goal-setting
11. Humor
    Ecclesiastes 3:4
12. Language

9. Control Your Language
    Proverbs 10:20 and 15:1, 28
10. Be Happy and Productive
    Ecclesiastes 7:18
11. Enjoy Every moment
12. Happiness is the Way
13. Make Good Use of Your Time
14. What You Can Dream - Begin
    Proverbs 29:18
15. Know When to Wait and Be Quiet
    Proverbs 13:3 and 21:23; James 1:19
16. Spend Time Alone Each Day
    Mark 1:35 and 6:31-32, 46
17. Do Unto Others as You Would Have Them Do Unto You
    Matthew 7:12; Luke 6:31
18. Do Unto Others as They Would Have You Do Unto Them
19. Be a Good Listener
    Ecclesiastes 5:1+; James 1:19
20. Be Nice to People
    *Romans 12:18, 20; Proverbs 11:17; and
    Philippians 2:3*
21. Smile and be Pleasant to Others
    Romans 12:10
22. Be Interested in Others
    Galatians 6:2; Proverbs 12:25
23. Avoid Negative People
    Proverbs 14:7
24. Avoid Win-Lose Situations
    Romans 12:9
25. Like Yourself
    Luke 10:27; Galatians 5:14
26. Ask and it Shall Be Given
    Seek and You Will Find
    Knock and it will Be Opened unto You
    Matthew 7:7; James 1:5
27. Steady Effort Brings Prosperity; Hasty Speculation
    Brings on Poverty
    Proverbs 21:5 and 28:20

APPENDIX II

Reference Material

1. *The Art of Talking So That People Will Listen* – Paul W. Swets

2. *The Eighty/20 Principle* – Richard Koch

3. *Is it Worth Dying For?* – Dr. Robert S. Eliot and Dennis L. Boreo

4. *Laugh and Learn* – Doni Tamblyn

5. *Leadership* – Rudolph W. Guiliani

6. Nightingale – Conant Corp. – audio material

7. *The 100 Secrets of Happy People* – David Niven, Ph.D.

8. *The One Minute Manager* – Kenneth Blanchard, PhD, and Spencer Johnson, MD

9. *The One to One Future* – Dan Pepper and Martha Rogers, Ph.D.

10. *Proverbs* (The Book of)

11. *Rich Dad Poor Dad* – Robert T. Kiyosaki with Sharon L. Lechter, CPA

12. *The Richest Man in Babylon* – George S. Clason

13. *The Science of God* – Gerald L. Schroeder

14. *The Secret of Success* – R. C. Allen

15. *Secrets of Power Persuasion*- Roger Dawson

16. *The Seven Habits of Highly Effective People* – Stephen R. Covey

17. The Teaching Company – visual material

18. www.askelm.com – spiritual material

NOTES

NOTES

NOTES

NOTES

NOTES

NOTES